"More people give me things to read than I can possibly keep up with but when I received your manuscript, I sat down and read it in two days.... I think you have some very good suggestions, and formulas... I shall be glad to recommend it to clients and friends.

Dr. Hazel M. Denning
founder of the Association
for Past Life Research & Therapy

"<u>Time</u> <u>Travel</u> has taught me how to open my mind and have fun. I was able to see what I've been looking for."

Meriko Makanishi

"A wonderful learning experience from an excellent teacher, I feel more open."

Neil Wada

elley Lessin Stockwell

Sex and Other Touchy Subjects

Insides Out

Smile On Your Face Money In Your Pocket: Do-It-Yourself Hypnosis

Denial Is Not A River In Egypt: Breaking Free From Addictions and Compulsions

<u>Audio Cassettes</u>

Yes I Can!

Peace and Calm

Sleep, Beautiful Sleep

Deep Into a Calming Ocean

Mommy Bunny's Going to Work

Lose Weight!

No More Sugar Junkie

Yes, You Can Quit Smoking

No More Alcohol

Great Golf

Time Travel

Sex and Other Touchy Subjects

Overcoming the Circle of Addiction

These and other books and tapes from Creativity Unlimited Press.
See order forms at the end of this book.

TIME TRAVEL

DO-IT-YOURSELF PAST LIFE JOURNEY HANDBOOK

By Shelley Lessin Stockwell

♡ CREATIVITY UNLIMITED PRESS

CREATIVITY UNLIMITED PRESS
30819 CASILINA
RANCHO PALOS VERDES, CA. 90274

ISBN 0912559-19-5
LIBRARY OF CONGRESS NUMBER 91-90382

PRINTED IN THE USA

DEDICATION

To my special friends who were the bridge taking this book from thought to form.

My heartfelt love and gratitude to Jon Nicholas, Sandra Kaneshiro, Jerry Duckett, Laura Waag, Dennis Briskin, Dr. Alex Lessin, Dr. Joan Kelly Lessin, Polly Englant, Bryce Stockwell, Nica Lee, Barbara McNurlin, Dr. Tom Rische, Jan Magdelano, Nina Wheeler, Ewa Carlsson, Don Bay and Ormond McGill. Your support made this book possible.

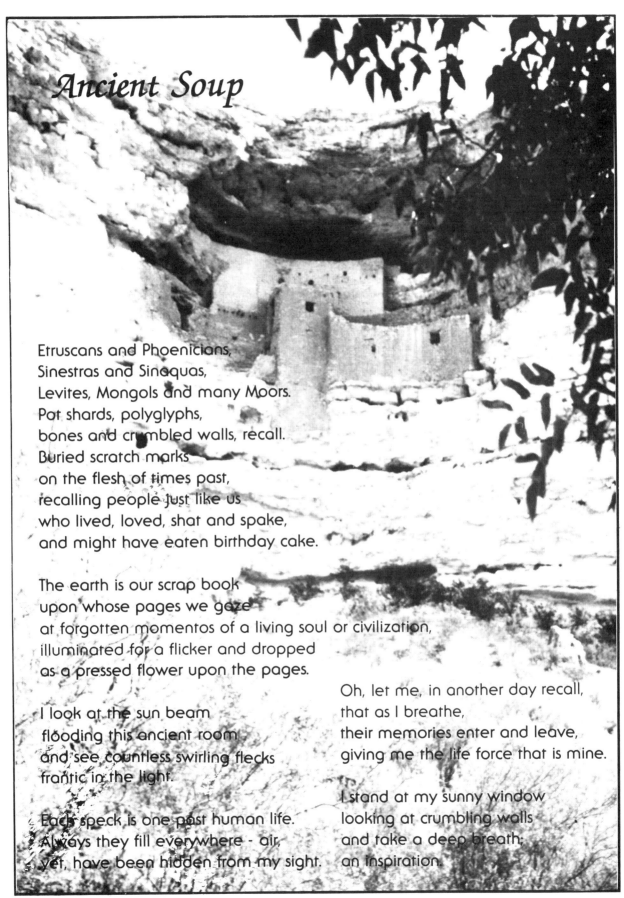

Ancient Soup

Etruscans and Phoenicians,
Sinestras and Sinaquas,
Levites, Mongols and many Moors.
Pot shards, polyglyphs,
bones and crumbled walls, recall.
Buried scratch marks
on the flesh of times past,
recalling people just like us
who lived, loved, shat and spake,
and might have eaten birthday cake.

The earth is our scrap book
upon whose pages we gaze
at forgotten momentos of a living soul or civilization,
illuminated for a flicker and dropped
as a pressed flower upon the pages.

I look at the sun beam
flooding this ancient room
and see countless swirling flecks
frantic in the light.

Each speck is one past human life.
Always they fill everywhere - air,
yet, have been hidden from my sight.

Oh, let me, in another day recall,
that as I breathe,
their memories enter and leave,
giving me the life force that is mine.

I stand at my sunny window
looking at crumbling walls
and take a deep breath:
an inspiration.

Photo by Jon Nicholas

PAST LIFE PREFACE

Have you ever been to a place for the first time and felt that you had been there before? Have you ever caught a glimpse of reality in a dream? Have you met someone new, yet, so familiar that you feel you've known them forever? Do certain cultures and peoples draw you to them while others leave you cold? What is deja vu?

This book is a map to the nature of your deepest perception. As you do each exercise you will remember the unlimited wonder that is you.

In the dawning of my 20's, I was walking along a small path at Esalan Institute in Big Sur, California. I heard two people talking in strange words. They spoke of "enlightenment experiences," and "transcending the earth plane." I did not know what they were talking about and yet their words had powerful pull for me.

For as long as I could remember (actually, for as long as I couldn't remember) I had been looking for the meaning of my life. Up to that moment, I thought the meaning of my life was to come from the things I did, from the outer values. Their words tapped a strange familiar feeling that I associated with an inner value; with being alive. In that moment, I realized that I was looking for my own "experience" of being alive. Thus, my quest for inner purpose sparked.

This book is about rejuvenation: how to feel the powerful ecstasy of your life force. You learn simple tools that let you experience being alive. Your life's purpose and bliss awaits. Use these powerful exercises to open countless doors into the sacred world of yourself. Wake up. Bring yourself back to your life now, in the past, and in the future. I hope to take the mystery out of getting there so you may swoon in the rapture of the mysteries you find.

It is with my heartfelt love and caring that I offer you this book.
I'd love to hear from you! You may contact me through my publisher:

Creativity Unlimited Press
30819 Casilina
Rancho Palos Verdes, CA 90274
(310) 541-4844

Bon Voyage!

Shelley Lessin Stockwell

FOREWORD

By Ormond McGill

Time Travel; Do-It-Yourself Past-Life Journey Handbook is a how-to book. How-to books are very popular because they show you how to do something. This book shows you how to travel backward in time to recall past-life experiences. You can even use this book to travel into the future!

Ever since H.G.Wells wrote "The Time Machine" mankind has fantasized about time travel. Now, Shelley Lessin Stockwell shows you how to do it by bringing awareness of past-lifetimes experiences into your consciousness. *Everything one experiences is through their consciousness of those experiences.*

Is mental time travel real? If it comes through to consciousness as an experience one has had in past time, it is fully as real as any other experience of which you become aware. Indeed, "time travel" experiences are frequently so profound they eclipse most experiences you have in the here and now.

To appreciate past-life experiencing is to appreciate the truth of reincarnation. Reincarnation accepts as fact that every living person in the entire world returns from death to live again and again, over and over. It is nature's way. At this moment something within you dies and something is reborn anew. Within seven years in your current lifetime, every cell in your body will be replaced, and you will be dwelling in an entirely different body than the one you wear right now. Yet, your stream of consciousness goes on uninterrupted. Your stream of consciousness is truly an immortal part of your SELF.

Even the stars follow this pattern. A star is born, it exists for eons of time, and then it dies (becoming a "black hole" in space). Further eons pass and it is reborn to shine with energy. The entire universe follows the pattern of reincarnation, and each person is a miniature of the universe.

Like the stars, we have all died many deaths before we came into our immediate incarnation. What we call birth is like one of the two sides of a door called "entrance" from the outside and "exit" from the inside.

If you say previous lifetimes don't exist because you have no conscious memory of them, consider what scientists tell us. Research proves that our every day perceptions are limited. There are, in fact, objects you cannot see, sounds you cannot hear, odors you cannot smell, tastes you cannot taste and vibrations you cannot feel. Yet, these sounds, smells, images and sensations are measurable. They exist in reality. You may not consciously remember your recent birth, yet no one doubts that you were born. In like manner, past life material exists beyond your daily perceptions.

Not many years ago evolution was a theory believed by few. Today, evolution is accepted by the majority. Evolution is the evolvement of the physical body. Reincarnation is the evolvement of the soul (the real YOU) that dwells within that body. Both are concurrent and interrelate to each other. Body after body, or more properly expressed, life experience after life experience must be engaged in for the growth of the soul.

Why?

We are here to learn. We are here to advance in consciousness.

Shelley Lessin Stockwell's "Time Travel" is a handbook teaching you to revive the forgotten memories of your past lives and how to explore your future lives as well. She writes as a technician, poet and historian of knowledge ancient and modern. What she writes about is amazingly complex yet remarkably simple.

Read this book carefully and then do what it tells you to do. Get aboard your personal time machine. You will be on your way to the greatest adventure of your life. Time Travel through your inner space connects directly with the vastness of outer space. The whole Cosmos is yours to experience and explore.

Ormond McGill
The Dean of American Hypnosis
Palo Alto, California
1991

Illustration by Jan Magdelano

Other Illustrations by   Jan Magdelano
Travis Walton
Nina Wheeler
Shelly Lessin Stockwell
Laura Montgomery Waag
Jeff Bucchino
Robin Cline
Photography by   Jon Nichols
Dennis Briskin

Cover Illustration by Jan Magdelano
Graphic Design by   Laura Montgomery Waag

"The path of earth is long. You have begun to remember now. There is a medicine bag that lies between the four quadrants of your brain matter: the Medicine Bag of Remembrance. You bring it to your quadrants now. You begin a balance of kinds.

The sun is the giver of energy. Mother Earth is the giver of life. You and the wingeds and four leggeds and water creatures are the threads between the two, honor both the sun and the earth or your time on the earth walk is shorter.

You have come to a time of opening, place your feet soundly on the earth as the standing people. Let the roots of your being feel the power of your mother. Let the branches of your being collect the light of your sisters and brothers.

You may close your eyes and find your medicine bundle between the four directions encased in the shell of your skull. Within your medicine bundle is the remembrance of your true nature.

You are separate, for you are a thread in the weaving of life. Without you, the tapestry is incomplete. You each have separate talents and colors and purpose. Notice your medicine now. you are but a visitor on this plane, yet you add a color like no other. I bless you."

by Red Feather
as channeled by Shelley
June 7, 1992

TABLE OF CONTENTS

Part I: THE JOURNEY

Part II: ACTION: DO IT

Return again. Return again.
Return to the land of your soul.
Return to what you are.
Return to who you are.
Return to where you are
Born
And reborn again.
Return again. Return again.
Return to the land of your soul.

-David Zeller

"The collective unconscious contains the whole spiritual
heritage of mankind's evolution, born anew in the brain
structure of every individual."

-Carl Jung

AN OVERVIEW

<u>TIME TRAVEL: DO-IT-YOURSELF PAST LIFE JOURNEY HANDBOOK</u> is divided into two parts. The first part gives you an idea of what to expect on your journey and the rules of the road. Part two are the road maps to get there.

This book will teach you 12 approaches to your inner self: each special and powerful in its own right. <u>You will learn</u> Hypno-Regression and the two special breath work techniques of Rebirthing and Holotropic Breathing. In addition, you will explore three vibrational approaches: the Shelley Stockwell Good Vibe System, the Egyptian System of Color and Symbols, and Taking Up Resonance: the Sound Approach. And you will be surprised and elated experiencing Automatic Writing, Ideomotor Conversations, Telepathy, and the Touch Approach.

Each style evokes a unique and special journey . Some will feel more comfortable than others since different techniques capitalize on different sensory preferences. I invite you to use each approach and see, hear, feel, taste, smell, and intuit what happens. If you are fit to listen to your truth, you will benefit from any of these journeys. If you are pregnant, have heart trouble or epilepsy, avoid doing the deep breathing exercises while alone. Work with a breathworker, rebirther, or hypnotherapist. If you are in pain, be it physical or emotional, understand that if you face pain directly it will release. If you feel depressed, know that the opposite of depression is expression. If you remain stuck, write down how you feel being stuck; call a friend; or go see a therapist or counselor.

Throughout history our ancestors have had enlightenment experiences on their own. We arrive alone, leave alone, and grow alone. The powerful flame of wisdom that lies within us makes the singular journey richer than an auditorium of therapists.

These exercises may be done alone or with someone. If you like to have someone hold your hand during your journey, a sensitive friend, hypnotherapist, or an individual who specializes in time travel would be terrific.Refer to page 18 (Traveling Companions) for help in selecting an appropriate guide and page 20 (Resource List) for a list of specialists.

Vivid examples of actual regressions and progressions induced, processed, and recorded using the same techniques you are learning, are at the end of each how to section.

Perhaps the most astounding part of this work is the personal benefit you receive in the here and now. You experience a resurgence of energy and motivation as you reach your goals and dream, improve your self esteem, relax, and feel in control of your life. These are all by-products of your trip. Say "goodbye" to headaches and insomnia and "hello" to better relationships with yourself and others.

Oriental philosophy claims that we each have some 800 lifetime memories stored within. May you never feel lonely again!

Illustration by Robin Cline

PART I:

THE
JOURNEY

THE FOUNDATION OF AN UNFORGETTABLE TRIP INTO MEMORY.

GETTING STARTED • FINDING YOUR WAY • WHAT TO EXPECT

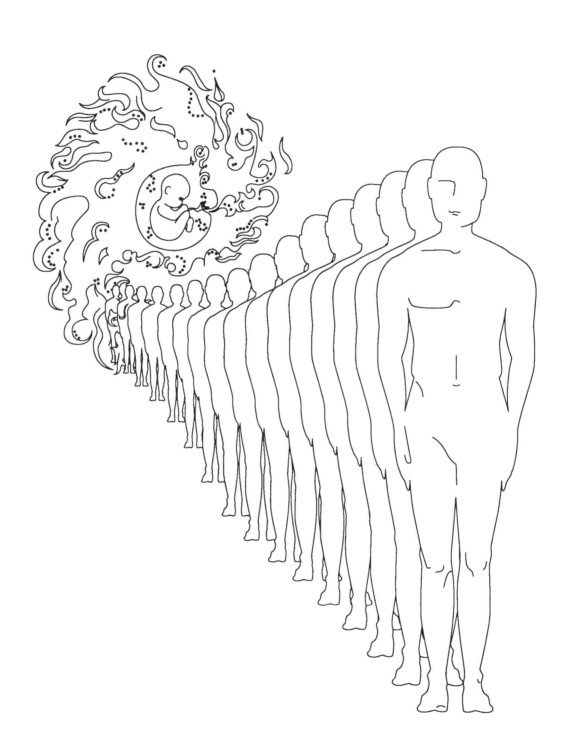

CHAPTER 1

RULES OF THE ROAD

The Best Cause
Be. Cause

BASIC RULES

If you were to enjoy a sightseeing trip in a car you would be sure that you knew how to drive that car. When you travel your precious inroads, you need to be sure that you know how to move yourself through the byways.

Four basic rules keep you moving and joyous:
    (1)   I TRUST MY JOURNEY
    (2)   I USE EVERYTHING TO MY BEST ADVANTAGE
    (3)   I TRUST MY SENSES
    (4)   I TRUST MY EMOTIONS

I TRUST MY JOURNEY

Whatever information is revealed, it presents you with an opportunity to improve the condition of your life right <u>now</u>. God or the higher spirit (as you envision him/her/it) at all times moves you toward joy and harmony. Each new awareness fills you with light.

You become in-lightened. New awareness leaves you feeling full (full-filled), whole and satisfied. You fall in love with your life. You are aware of your personal destiny and place in the universe. As you evolve and grow and become aware of this feeling of wholeness, you experience a profound sense of personal satisfaction.

My many clients express vivid detailed images of other lives and other times. All information is always relevant to each individual's self love and happiness in the here and now.

I USE EVERYTHING TO MY BEST ADVANTAGE

This book is for you. The more you learn, the more direction and clarity you will bring to living. Take advantage of knowing everything you can. You deserve it!

I TRUST MY SENSES

There is a part of you that knows that if you trust your senses; they will never lie. Your senses offer you health on all levels: psychic, mental, spiritual, emotional, and physical. Your body tells you of any problem areas and offers you the cure. This information is always there if you choose to listen. Occasionally, people experience psychic awareness during a journey. Enjoy one if it occurs!

Russell Targ and Harold Puthoff at Stanford's Research Institute proved that everyone is psychic if they simply trust the impressions they receive. Subjects told that they had "permission" to be psychic were.

I TRUST MY EMOTIONS

Deeply emotional experiences, when expressed, give a tremendous feeling of relief. Laughter, as well as crying, are powerful ways to discharge stored tension and that heals us. If any emotion comes up; invite its release. Holding back feelings literally dams up your nervous system, clogs your clarity and blocks your self loving.

Say these four affirmations out loud:

> I Trust My Journey
> I Use Everything to My Best Advantage
> I Trust My Senses
> I Trust My Emotions

WHAT WILL YOU FIND?

The journey is the destination.
Find and ye shall seek.

Expect to feel relaxed and comfortable. All of these processes bring inner peace. The form the journey takes varies each time you depart and explore. Just let it be. I personally have accessed lives of men, women, and animals. I even had a client who was a granite boulder who transformed as a result of volcanic activity. Avoid any expectations at all. Be open and see, hear, taste, and touch what you find.

If you are afraid that you will lose control and feel helpless, understand that you take control of your control when you make a choice to relinquish control. You are always in control. Anytime you want to, you can open your eyes and return to your present awareness.

Carl Jung said: "In the center of every fear is a desire."

PROGRESSIONS

Though this book focuses on *Regressions* (past visions), it is quite possible to explore progressions (future visions). You may investigate forward thinking by altering each exercise to request your deepest mind to move into the future: tomorrow, next year or into a future life time.

Here is an example of my first progression:

2074

His name is Kali. Their house is in the earth. Houses are like that. 2074. Huts. They look like Eskimo huts. The air is dead. Lost its energy but it is healthy now. No more bacteria. The nervous system has changed a little. Lungs breathe differently. The cilia on the lungs no longer look like hair. It is thicker and filters better. The air got dead. Everything is cleaner now. Zap the air. Sprogan. Sprogan emits a beam of energy and neutralizes bacteria. Works in water, in air and even on a person. It's not a good idea to use it on a person. It makes them flat and dead. They lose their vitality when you sprogan a person. I saw people sproganed. They look sick.

We wear funny hats. Flat in front and shot up in the back. It's like a solid wing on your head. It pulls in energy from the sun. It is our own private energy conversion unit.

For vacation, we like to lie down on doak mobiles. The doak mobiles are little chairs with no legs and they float. Some say they don't really float or fly, that it is just altered-consciousness. I believe you do fly. They named them from the old phrase "okie dokie" - doak mobiles. Kind of an oak joke.

My color is green. I work on green strata. I help people with nourishment. I am experimenting now with molds and fungi. My name is Dilja Gorman. I am 27 years old. I was born in the alloy flat room. I was supposed to be used in the outer work but I chose the green level. The outer work goes to other planets. Green level stays here.

I like to visit my mother and father in the "earthy igloo" I call it. My brother, John is 18. (actually Alex, Shelley's brother) My mother is Carmen (really Steve, Shelley's first love) and my father is Joseph. He is a serious man and he needs to be. He works in the outer circles. Very tense work. You must think very much.Earth is divided into 6 realms. I hope the green belt reaches all of them. If people are nourished properly, they will never fight wars again.

Many people have died when Earth became sterile. That will never happen again as long as there is a green belt. My work is my life. I am proud to be in the green belt.

It is 2085 and I transition and evaporate.

REGRESSIONS

Your story may unfold in bits and pieces and in jumbled sequence. For example, in 1986 during a regression, I met my first American Indian "Red Feather." After that I relived 14 other "lives" of diverse animals and humans. The 15th regression brought me "Broken Cloud" who revealed more about "Red Feather" and the tragic death of his son. In 1990 (4 years later), while using my self directed movie technique, I met "Screaming Eagle" ("Broken Cloud's" father) who told me a fuller, more detailed account of "Red Feather" and his murdered son "Little Eagle." I also have "met" in recent regressions, the wife of Little Eagle's murderer and other witnesses.

The installments accurately supported and expounded upon the previous information yet I saw them out of order.

Here are three Native American journeys arranged in linear time:

Red Feather (1986 - Accessed using Touch Approach)

Large, elder Indian male, one red feather with white tip, looking, grieving over the ashes of his son slaughtered here on the earth. He burned him and is grieved. A senseless death.

I was a good Indian and worshiped the sun and loved my son and he was massacred for no just reason.

(send him the light)
I see a staircase going to the sun. A hallway of sunlight. I know who is waiting for me at the end - God. I've met her before.

Screaming Eagle (1990 - Accessed using Self Directed Movie Approach)

I stand upon the hill. Eagle feathers upon my arms. My arms are outstretched, reaching..reaching..like the eagle, reaching upward to touch the sky, to visit the sun. The sun is all knowing. Screaming Eagle. I am Screaming Eagle. I have learned to fly and touch the sky and visit the sun.

Now the sun has gone dark. My eyes have become blind. Into my heart, a gray cloud, darker, darker. Darker then the logs that burned in the fire. Darker then the boy whose skull is in the ashes. The fire cooks the brains from the skull until it melts. Seeps deep. Deep, as the dry river bed where water used to flow. The boy had black hair. The boy was brave. The sun gave him to the people. The boy had eyes made of the sun. From the ground, the earth - Earth eyes with sun. Moving toward all he saw.

We kneeled before the boy for we knew that he was given to us as a blessing to lead us back. Back to the antelope, back to the bear, back to the lush, green river. Back to the red cliffs. He climbs the ladder to the cliff and we all follow him with our eyes. The boy is Gregory. We call him, not Gregory, we call him Little Eagle.

The Indians come. Apache. Broken Bow. Dakota. Gyayan and the Onitaka (with their red blankets like red hills). The boy speaks with his eyes. We sit around the fire. Many peoples, many tribes, many ways. Some smoking long pipes with eagle feathers. Some on horse. Some dragging children behind on wooden sticks. Some with papoose strapped tight to bosom or back. I see the boy - Eagle boy. When you look at Eagle boy, he enters you and you feel him in your eyes, in your ears, in your nose, upon your mouth, right down the middle, into your back and right into your stomach and right out from where the cord is strong. The boy weaves us, from cord to cord, all tribes, all people, all one.

The boy is dead. Blackened in the fire. Blackened with the people's hearts, their eyes, ears, nose and lips. The sun will not shine. Great sadness.

The land is dusty and parched and we will all die as we lived. The boy has been killed. Big Bear killed him. Threw a rock upon his head. Big Bear was very angry and not of all mind and the boy loved him with his last breath.
The goddess welcomed him, coming from the light. "Come brave".

(what did Shelley learn from this entity?)
I have learned many lessons from Screaming Eagle. I must learn to remove the black hole and become the boy. I am the boy. I was born with that boy in my heart.

(send him the light)
I send the boy white light and he smiles.

Broken Cloud (1986 - Accessed using Touch Approach)

Now listen to me. Eagle feathers on my arms. I stand on the hill. I am wise. And they all come to hear. They think I am powerful because I listen to the sky. And the clouds and the sun and the eagle. I listen well and they ask me. I tell them what they need to know. I am head of the tribe. Broken Cloud is my name. I am very wise Apache. I am as wise as my father-Screaming Eagle. My mother - White Doe - she wore buckskin fringe.

I couldn't do it when I was a boy. I couldn't do it. I had to learn. I doubted I could learn. I had to learn to trust the sky and sun. I didn't believe I could trust the sun again. I was afraid to have a son because of Red Feather. My father said I must be Chief. My father made me go alone in the wilderness for two weeks and I cried for half. I died and woke. And I trusted. I was like the rattlesnake. Sheds his skin. I had to shed Red Feather. His boy was massacred. I carried Red Feather in my heart and gut. He is brown and wrinkled and sad. He has eyes like brown beads and he has white hair.

(send him the light)
As I send him the light, he becomes my father. His eyes look wide and big - radiant - the light comes through his eyes. He is happy. The light comes through his eyes. He soaks in the light like Earth soaks rain.

I love Red Feather. Red Feather is my soul. I am always Red Feather. Red Feather loves the light. Has a deep sorrow when the light betrayed him. Worshiped sun, light then they massacred his boy. He went back to the light when he died and kept some sorrow and grief for me. The sun has always been there emanating truth. Your soul is learning to return fully in light. You must learn to forgive and to not fear. What goes around comes around.

I always return to the light. There is a God: dwells in the light, plants, my heart, the light. In the earth, the animals and in all other humans and all other reincarnations.

Trust the light,
keep looking
keep opening,
keep trusting the light.

For the last 20 years I have collected some 300 ceramic turtles. Imagine my delight to access the following regression.

Tortoise

Mountains are here - can't see them - it's dark but I can feel them. Very still. Everything has to be with nature. I am part of nature - not a person - scallops on top of white fence. White architecture. Scallops. lots of intricate white scallops around everything - white washed earth walls.

Animals in fields, four legs, big fur, and me - I'm little. I don't move much - no feet. I'm a turtle. Sit under my shell. Green and black shell a little yellow on the inside. I don't move very much - I'm very old. Very heavy - tired and peaceful (been in this place a long time) I like it here. Bottom of houses - scallops on fences. I smell them. They smell like earth. I've been a turtle for a long time. Long as I can remember. Maybe I was an eagle once, I'm not sure.

I'm too heavy to know
I like to show
Everything seeps in that way
as it seeps in I get heavier
and richer, slower, and wiser
I am very wise and very slow.

I know about eagles. A wind is blowing now, wind blows through my shell; making music in here. I hide food in here with me. There's a cat I don't like, that's all.

SPIRITUAL ENCOUNTERS

As you transcend time, you will eventually have mystical experiences. Mystical experiences are the raisins on the wheat bread of life. Here time is not ordered sequentially and you will transcend time and space arriving in an eternal now. If you feel lost as you read these words, know that when you enter into this realm you will understand. Mystical experiences transcend words.

Golden Lady

My goal this lifetime - my purpose is to trust myself as God. That's all I have. Nothing else to prove.

I'm back in the sun. It's now. I'm a woman. I make love, I am schooled in making love. I reach God. I wear gold fabric draping. I am very beautiful. I am stroked and feathered. Many servants, born of God. I have dark skin - dark hair. I make love for God, My birthright. I am very peaceful, very peaceful, very whole.

I am massaged. I am flowered. I am painted. I am beautiful. I give all food, all money to people below me. I treat my servants with respect. I do not permit them to bow to me. I give to them and they give devotion. And god speaks. When I hear him I till my father. He listens to my words from God. I do not abuse that. I do not stand in the way of God. He speaks to me and I am love and I love.

I die very suddenly, my heart suddenly stops because God calls. I am not ready. I am very surprised. I'm very young. I go back to God. They package me in body and build a big pyramid but my body is not important. My father is very sad that I have died (my real father now).

I am blinded by the light.
My heart is full of the light
coming in, shining out.

I want to return to God, so full of love. My heart is so full.

God

I am God. I have no face. I have robes. I sit in the sun - I am part of the greatest God - I work and live in their reflection. I am God - my job here is to help people know that it is time to be born or time to come back. That's my job - I like it. Every day with joy - I've been here a long time.

Beams of light shooting down all around. Earth others here with white robes melting in the sun, don't always show. Meet and who again. The ones that show are ready to be born. I see one now... a lady - Gloria - doesn't have a face yet - doesn't want to be born yet - she will be born soon. I have hands that disappear like lights. I have wings and I fly. Or I sit or I fly and sit at the same time. Hard to say. I like Gloria - she'll make a fine human.

WHERE DO THESE IMAGES COME FROM?

When people hear of my past life work they inevitably say "Oh, you must believe in reincarnation." "I'm not sure", I respond. Philosophers have been speculating on the source of this information as everything from keen imagination and reincarnation to Jung's theory of the collective unconscious.

I do know that any person who accesses the subconscious mind using any of the techniques in this book, will retrieve and revivify powerful scenarios of other people, places and times. We are each a product of genetics. My friend was born with a white streak in the front of her black hair, a striking characteristic that her mother had as well. When her child was born, she too sported that same white lock of hair. From our ancestors we have learned to walk upright. Since every cell in our body is an identical genetically coded replica of every other cell. It seems reasonable to assume that each cell also carries detailed information about the lives of our ancestors.

How little is known of our human minds. A mind understanding itself is a heartbeat away from our grasp. So where do these images come from? I am not sure. What good do these images do for us? I know fully. Each recall brings us into a more intimate harmony with ourselves, our life's purpose and all humankind.

THE TRUTH SHALL SET YOU FREE

A molecule moving
in the dark of night
Silently entering
beyond our sight
Surging and moving
in a rhythm of heart
We are the whole
We are a part.

Images of remembered lives are like holograms. You may look at them from various angles and perspectives and they'll change in impact, hue, and intensity.

Each image is an overlay to your life in the present. You will be amazed how this composite image helps you take back control of your actions in the "now". When you are unconsciously influenced by an event, you act to recreate it or avoid it. Both of these re-actions determine your action. When you return to the source of your re-action, you empower yourself with a choice. You no longer need to behave "because of" or "in spite of". Your action is a decision based on your clarity and free will.

You may selectively remember or forget parts of your journey. That's just fine. In the process of allowing the memories to surface and be expressed, you release past pain, hurt or trauma and evoke healing, understanding, and integration in your life in the here and now. Keep doing regressions, progressions, and mystical journeys, each time saying to yourself "I will remember" and you will. As you practice you recall more.

Opening yourself is a peeling.

The only way out is through.

Occasionally, we block our expanding awareness with anxiety. If this happens it is a delicious opportunity to break through old limits. Breaking the fear barrier during your journey will become a powerful metaphor of personal freedom in your life in the here and now.

If you experience a mental or physical block during any of these processes, *Do not quit !* Place your breathing, your energy, and your focus into that block. Amplify it. Magnify it. Stay with it and it will release. Focus white light upon a stuck image and notice what happens next. If, for example, you have accessed a past life in England and seem to be frozen in one scenario, let's say you are a 10 year old chap, magnify the event or details of that image. Breathe there and send that 10 year old white light. Notice every detail. Use all your senses. Then ask; "What happens next" and notice. Then take a deep cleansing breath.

If you feel frightened, look into the eyes of the "monster" and ask; "What is troubling you?". Use all your senses as you experience the response. Or you may say; " I forgive you.". Stay with the negative and it always positively blossoms into a healing. The next chapter, Chapter 2 are list of several other ways to achieve closure. Listed under *Happy Endings* each question lets you connect with your vision, learn your lessons, and release any upset with love.

Now that you have learned the general guidelines of time travel, let us map your course for each special style of trance-portation.

CHAPTER 2

RULES FOR EACH JOURNEY: MAPPING YOUR COURSE

I am a part of all I meet
From my wrinkled brow
to my flat little feet
When you walk a path with me
I carry along a part of thee.

You add focus and direction
As we proceed in our procession

If you are jagged or divisive
Hurtful, cold, detached, derisive;
If you are kind, smooth, honest, clear,
Generous, lusty, or love me dear:

I will take what you will show
And, with it, I will shape and grow
Becoming who I am to be
As you become a part of me.

Although there are many techniques to open the door to the "inner room of your mind", they all share the same important guidelines. Your goal, the music, blessings, grounding techniques, or having a friend hold your hand, all enhance the trip.

THE PURPOSE OF YOUR JOURNEY

Decide what it is that you would like to know, explore, or clarify before you begin. Are you going back in time (regressions)? Would you like to explore your birth, past lives, or the source of an issue or pain? Are you tracking someone else to see what your relationship was in another place in time? Are you going into the future (progressions)? How far into the future? Next week? Next month? Five years from now? 100 years? Are you looking for a spiritual awakening or an encounter with an inner guide? Are you choosing to heal an illness or alter a pattern of behavior that does not serve you well? Or, you may decide not to decide and go anywhere the journey takes you. Whatever you choose, it will be perfect.

Once you plan your course, you may begin.

MUSIC

Music is a proven stimuli to bring about altered consciousness. Choose to play music that is soothing, repetitious, and something you enjoy. I believe it is a good idea to avoid vocals or words and, especially, to stay away from music that entices you to sing along. Let the music be a back drop and not the focal point.

MUSIC LIST:
This is some of my favorite traveling music. You might enjoy the new age music section of your store and discover your own favorites.

Deep Into A Calming Ocean by Allen Kaufman; Creativity Unlimited,
    30819 Casilina Drive, Rancho Palos Verdes, Ca. 90274
    Induces alpha state subtly and beautifully.

Path Of Joy (and anything else) by Daniel Kobialka; Arkay Records, San Jose, CA.
    Perfect lilting music.

Ice Flowers Melting by Sylvan Grey; Fortuna Records, Novato, CA.
    Meditative music played on the Finnish folk heart.

Cuzco by Aperlimac
    Try it, you'll like it. Uplifting

BLESS ME, BLISS ME

Each process starts with a "blessing". A blessings is the chance for you to make a spiritual reconnection with God, Nature, or a Higher Power as you envision Him/Her/It. Ask for guidance, protection, clarity, and growth. This gentle prayer feels good, centers you, and it keeps these processes on the highest level.

> Bless me on all levels
> Physically, mentally
> Emotionally and spiritually
> So I may truly
> recognize and fulfill my life's purpose.
> Let all teachings be for the highest good
> of myself and humanity.
> Help me reconnect
> with my special gifts
> and let me lovingly shed any
> negative messages given by insensitive people.
>
> Thank you.
> Amen.

TAPE RECORDING

A wonderful way to capture your visions, experiences, and travels is by using a tape recorder. Make sure you have fresh batteries (or that it is plugged in) and put a new tape inside. 45 minute tapes work well. Then, as the images present themselves, report them out loud. Later, when you return to your present awareness, you may listen to the message and write it down on paper. That is how many of the past life journeys in this book were captured. If you do not have a tape recorder, scribe your experience on paper (using words or drawings) as soon as you complete each trip. If you have a traveling companion ask them to "scribe" for you, writing down your words.

JOURNEY QUESTIONS

During each time travel experience, be it a regression or progression, answer the following questions. They will clarify and complete your journey. If you forget to ask any of the questions, that's fine. Do it on the next journey. If at all possible, be the person or image from your vision and answer the questions from their personal viewpoint. Not all answers may make sense to you or be logical. You needn't think or analyze. Just ask each question and let the answer emerge.

- **•Feet?**
  Look at your feet. This will ground you. Describe what you see. Notice if you have shoes. If you do not perceive feet or body that is fine too. You might be an energy or light being in this journey.

- **•Clothes?**
  Notice what you are wearing or not wearing.

- **•Senses?**
  One by one, allow your experience to enter each of your senses. Notice any smells, tastes, sounds, bodily sensations, sights and extra sensory sensations.

- **•Others?**
  Are you alone or with someone?

- **•Location?**
  Are you inside or outside?

- **•Time?**
  What is the time period or year? What season is it?

- **•Experience?**
  What is happening? What happens next?

- **•Death?**
  Answer the question: "How did this entity die?"

- **•White Light**
  Send that entity white light. Picture and imagine a flood of white light upon them and see what happens.

- **•Learned?**
  "What have I learned from this lifetime" or "What message is this entity wishing to give me?"

Once in a while, the past life that you access will have an "Other Worldly" energy. The "image" may come to you through any or all of your senses. Some experience them as moving fields of energy, colors, apparitions, or extra ordinaries. Sometimes the "happy Ending" questions simply do not match the material you access. Trust your intuition. Create questions that fit. In any event, if at all possible, ask what it is you need to learn from this experience.

MANDALAS

Teacher: "What are you drawing?"
Child: "I'm drawing a picture of God."
Teacher: "But no one knows what God looks like."
Child: "They will when I'm done."

Drawing a mandala is an exciting way to capture your journeys on paper. Get a large piece of paper and draw a circle about the size of a 78 record. (Remember those?) Have marking pens, crayons, or colored pencils available so that as soon as you finish your process, you may go to your paper and draw a picture of your experience. It is important that while you draw the picture, you do not think or analyze. This is not an exercise in art. Let the colors create the image. When you are done drawing, you might want to write down words to describe what the drawing means to you. You might like to tell someone about your drawing. I like to put my mandalas on the wall one next to the other. Over time, their beauty takes on new understanding and meaning for me. I particularly enjoy looking at them in sequential order. I think you will too.

AFTER THE JOURNEY: GROUNDING TECHNIQUES

The power of these journeys is enormous. When you alter your consciousness in this amazing way, you might feel temporarily disoriented or "spaced". Therefore, it is important that you "ground yourself" and reconnect to your clarity in the here and now so you can go about the tasks that make you functional in our modern world. If my grounding techniques seem peculiar to you, that is fine with me. DO THEM ANYWAY. They will balance your entire experience.

Touch the Earth
Walk barefoot on the grass, in the sand, or on the beach for twenty minutes. If it is too cold outside, walk barefoot (or in your stocking feet) on the floor of your house. Scrub the floor. Literally, get grounded. If you like working in the garden, put your hands in the soil, plant something, weed something. Mow the lawn. Do anything that lets you reconnect with nature and, particularly, the earth.

Vinegar Bath
Fill up your bathtub with warm water and add two cups of apple cider vinegar. Get the bathtub and submerge your head. Make sure to get your head and your entire body in the vinegar bath. A 15 minute soak is recommended.

Sleep
If at all possible, go to sleep for the night. If not, simply relax for a few minutes, undisturbed.

WHAT HAPPENS IF NOTHING HAPPENS?

When the student is ready, the teacher appears.

Don't worry. Something always happens. If you do not have a vivid past life image, that's fine. Enjoy what comes up and try another process the next time. Wherever your heart leads you is where you need to be. Past life images are there, ready to be accessed when you are ready to receive them. Just stay with these exercises. Regressions and progressions are *learned* skills that get better with practice.

If you sometimes think of yourself as a failure consider this: You are a successful person. The proof that you are successful is that you are reading this book. Successful people are open to learning.

If you sometimes think of yourself as plain or boring when you compare yourself to "other" beautiful people, consider this: You are a beautiful person. The proof that you are beautiful is that you are able to see the beauty in others. We are each mirrors for each other. Another's beauty is your own reflection or you would never see it.

TRAVELING COMPANIONS: I WANT TO HOLD YOUR HAND

If you would like a guide to share and support you on your journey, you might choose a sensitive friend or a professional who specializes in time travel to sit with you. Your own personal "sitter".

Choosing a Friend Quiz

You can maximize your experience by choosing a buddy who scores 100% true on this quiz:

1.	I like this person	T	F
2.	This person likes and respects me.	T	F
3.	This person acts kindly towards me.	T	F
4.	I feel safe with this person.	T	F
5.	This person is someone I have been able to discuss my feelings with before.	T	F

If you answered "True" to all these questions, you will be choosing someone who is most likely to be supportive.

What to Tell Your Chosen Friend

Ask your friend if they are willing to put aside time to be your guide. Some friends like to trade jobs. You might serve as support and guide for the first hour and then switch and take the journey yourself while your friend becomes your guide. It is important that you both:

- Agree to a time and place for the journey without any distractions

- Communicate how you would like to be supported.
    - Are there responses you want to hear or don't want to hear?
    - Do you want a good listener, someone to ask questions, or give suggestions?
    - Do you want to be held or touched or not touched at all?
    - Do you want them to keep your experiences confidential?
    - Do you want them to write down what you say or use a tape or video recorder?

Tell your guide what you would like or give them permission to intuit what to do for you. Talk to them first. Remember, that supportive people want to help yet, often don't know how and, even more often don't ask. They will welcome your guidance.

If You Are the Chosen Friend

If you are the sitter, your job is to be your partner's loving friend. When asked, wipe her brow if she perspires, stroke her forehead, hold her hand, blow her nose, generally protect and support her in her process. Remain nonverbal, unless you receive a transmission that she needs some guidance. If she says: "Stop!". Stop whatever it is you are doing. Remember that regardless of what your partner is doing, whether it be laughing, crying or moving, it is simply an outward expression of an inward awareness. Make sure to support her in that expression and not stifle her. If a past life emerges verbally, scribe for her; write it down.

Choosing a Professional Quiz

You can maximize your experience by choosing a professional who scores 100% true on this quiz. The title of the professional you choose may be varied: hypnotherapists, acupuncturists, rolfers, shiatsu, masseurs, rebirthers, Grof breathworkers. Most important is not the title but the mind set. Be sure this person seems sensitive, clean, sober, and respectful of time travel.

1.	I like this person	T	F
2.	This person likes and respects me.	T	F
3.	This person acts kindly towards me.	T	F
4.	I feel safe with this person.	T	F
5.	This person respects the value of time travel.	T	F
6.	This person is in my price range.	T	F

If you answered "true" to all these questions, you will be choosing someone who is most likely to be supportive.

RESOURCE LIST:

Creativity Learning Institute

I conduct personal guided journeys and time travel seminars using the techniques in this book at my learning center in Rancho Palos Verdes, California. You may contact me at:

> Creativity learning Institute
> Shelley Stockwell, Dean
> 30819 Casilina
> Rancho Palos Verdes, CA 90274.
> Phone number: (310) 541-4844.

Breathworkers

Doctors Joan and Alexander Lessin are Grof Certified Holotropic Breathworkers. They work with individuals and with groups and offer a holotropic referral service. Their practice is on the beautiful island of Maui. You may contact them:

> Route 1 Box 166
> Wailuku, HI 96793.
> Phone Number: (808) 244-4103

Touch workers:

Trager practitioner Kathleen Zuhde is the head of "The Healing Center" in Hermosa Beach, CA. She may be contacted at (213) 376-7729.

Past Life Therapy Association:

This organization has some 700 members and offers a referral service.

> APART
> P.O. Box 20151
> Riverside, CA 92516
> Phone Number (714) 784-1570

READING LIST:

Though many time travel books are slanted and tend to withhold the actual techniques for regressions and progressions, there are a few fine ones. It is worthwhile to read them because you inspire yourself.

<u>Past Lives Future Lives</u> by Dr. Bruce Goldberg, 1982; New York; Ballantine Books.
Fascinating case studies of other's progressions and regressions.

<u>Other Lives, Other Selves</u> by Roger Woolger Ph.D., 1987; Bantam Books.
This is perhaps the best book of its kind. Dr. Woolger is a Jungian analyst who thoroughly explores the meaning of time travel. Highly recommended.

<u>Life Before Life</u> by Helen Wambach, 1979; Bantam Books.
Written by a hypnotist who toured the country hypnotizing hundreds. One of my favorites.

<u>Life After Life</u> and <u>Reflections of Life After Life</u> by Raymond A. Moody, Jr. M.D., 1977; Bantam Books.
Written by Helen Wambach's student, these books continue Wambach's investigations. Includes interviews with men and women who actually were pronounced "dead" but survived.

<u>On Death and Dying</u> by Elizabeth Kubler-Ross; 1969; New York, McMillan.
Kubler-Ross's profound study of people who were pronounced dead and lived to tell about it.

<u>The Adventure of Self Discovery</u> by S.& C. Grof; 1980; London: Thames & Hudson.
Intellectual yet fascinating.

<u>Heading Toward Omega: Life At Death</u> by Kenneth Ring; 1984; New York; William Morrow.
Society and individual views of the near death experience.

<u>Creative Mythology: The Masks of God</u> by Joseph Cambell; 1968; New York; Penguin Books.
Intellectual and powerful, Joseph Cambell is heady reading. Any of his books on mythology will intrigue you.

<u>Past Life Regression Guidebook</u> and <u>Past Lives Present Karma</u> by Bettye Binder; 1988 Culver City, Ca.; Reincarnation Books.
Accessible and Loving How-To Manuals. I find her focus upon distinguishing imagination from truth distracting, unnecessary and confusing. Still, they are fine books.

CHAPTER 3

PROCESSES OF ENLIGHTENMENT

May you live in rapture forever after.

En•light•en: ....to give spiritual insight to.

Enlightenment: ...18th century philosophical movement with emphasis on ideas of universal human progress and the free use of reason.

"Are you God?", she asked the Great Buddha.
"No, I am just awake", he answered.

As we alter our normal consciousness, our journey may move into the amazing realm of a transcendental states of awareness:
- The Kundalini Process of Enlightenment and
- Non-Ordinary States of Consciousness.

THE KUNDALINI

The kundalini is a form of energy associated with that feeling of being alive - filled with freely moving energy - flooded with light, or enlightenment. The kundalini process is a first hand experience of a person's physical body opening through the central nervous system via the spine and each of the seven chakras (base of spine, sexual organs, solar plexus, heart, throat, third eye, top of head) coupled with releasing of emotional or karmic "blocks".

Experiencing the kundalini is an ongoing process lasting from several months to many years. As the energy moves through the body it clears away blocking impurities or imbalances and leaves one with an experience of being fully alive; reborn or reawakened into a full feeling (fulfilling) experience of resonating energy. Joseph Cambell called it "feeling the rapture of being alive".

The sanskrit word, "kundalini", was used by the ancient Yogis as far back as 7000 years ago. They believed that without the kundalini energy, no enlightenment was possible. "The kundalini", they said, "is the central energy of all life". At death this "energy cocoon" leaves the body and determines the nature of each reincarnation

The patterns of movement, as energy travels through the body, varies slightly from culture to culture, yet, every pattern corresponds to the central nervous system. All agree that, as the different centers are activated, the spiritual awakening of that person intensifies.

Those who have experienced the kundalini have done so spontaneously, often as a result of a key event such as a near death experience or child birth. Kundalini awakening can also be stimulated by acupuncture, energy balancing, meditation, rolfing, touch therapies, and many of the awareness techniques in this book. Learning to contact and express your truth often stimulates the kundalini also. As you tell the truth to yourself and others, you realize your human potential. Human potential includes an amazing spirituality and a feeling of "God" energy.

The process of enlightenment can be quite dramatic and a person who is having a spiritual emergency might be inaccurately labeled (by those who do not understand) as being certifiably psychotic. This puts a kundalini soul in a peculiar dilemma. Their "spirit body" is being profoundly lifted into the sacred hand of God while their physical self might be chastised, exorcised, or even committed!

Fortunately today, there is a renaissance of truth and introspection as we collectively embark on the kundalini journey of an awakened world.

Since an enlightenment experience in the form of the kundalini process might be stimulated while doing many of the exercises in this book; particularly while using breathwork and vibrational techniques, it is helpful to be aware of what it might look and feel like.

As the chakras clear and open releasing freely moving energy, a person is often flooded with a myriad of physical and emotional experiences. These vary greatly from person to person.

THE SIGNPOSTS OF THE KUNDALINI

Are you experiencing the Kundalini?

If you have or are experiencing any of these objective or subjective signposts, know that you are being blessed with purification and balancing. The results will be greater emotional stability, enhanced intuition and a feeling of peace.

Body Sensations: Deep ecstatic tingling vibration feeling of orgasm Feeling hot and cold Visions of inner light	Actually seeing light internally or having an "Aha!" experience
Hearing sounds	Hearing strong sounds and voices seemingly from the inside.
Feeling Discomfort	Headaches or focused sensations in any region of the body. Beginning and ending abruptly.
Time Distortion	Thoughts speed up, slow down or stop. Spontaneous trance states.
Visual Balancing	The experience of simultaneously seeing the inner and outer.
Emotional Sensations: Detachment	A feeling of watching yourself.
Out of Body Experience	Feeling that you're away from your physical body
Intense emotions	Ecstasy, bliss and cosmic harmony. Occasionally fear, anger, depression, confusion followed by peace, love and contentment.
Psychic Abilities: Increased ESP Increased Intuitive Powers Ability to see Auras	Natural psychics are more likely to have a kundalini awakening.
Temporary Paralysis	Involuntary positioning of body, limbs or fingers.

NON-ORDINARY STATES GUIDE GROWTH
by Alexander Lessin, Ph.D.

Sometimes you will enter a NOS: a Non-Ordinary State of Consciousness. (Non (N) + ordinary (O) + State (S) = NOS.)

In it, you may love and feel oneness with all people and things; have peak experiences. You can get body rushes and visions. You could rerun repressed memories. Often, in a NOS, you relive womb-life, labor and birth. You may imagine past lives, sense psychic powers, see synchronicities.

Sometimes, in a NOS, you feel like you die. Then you meet light-beings and return – changed for the better – to everyday life. You may feel your ideas of yourself and the world die. Maybe you meet archetypal guides or gods. You could even sense yourself and everything in the cosmos as aspects of the Creative Force.

NOSs sometimes flood you without warning. You lower the floodgates to them when you stress yourself physically or emotionally. Illness, accident, intense sex, birthing, psychedelics can also open gates to unexpected NOSs. So can almost dying.

You prompt NOSs if you meditate or use hypnosis, practice holotropic or yogic breathing. Touch, see or contemplate a saint, beloved person or nature and you open yourself to NOSs. If you consider music, art, philosophy or quantum physics, you could induce a NOS.

Warning: Non-ordinary states upset you if you let them disrupt ordinary ones. NOSs also can upset certain people; if you share your NOSs with them, they may think you're crazy and get you confined and sedated.

Instead, share you NOSs with a spiritually-oriented friend or counselor.Let your counselor hear, watch, and hold you, give you healing love while you work through the hurts of your life, birth and fantasy. You conjure healing archetypes, have mystical reactions.

The visions, feelings and insights you get from a NOS will free you, make you more present. Cleansed, you drop grandiose drives. You empathize more, enjoy people's differences. And relish nature. Your NOSs let you view yourself and your experiences as part of a divine plan.

RESOURCE LIST:

<u>Kundalini</u> <u>Psychosis</u> <u>or</u> <u>Transcendence</u> by Dr. Lee Sanella MD, 1978;
    H.S. Dankin Company; San Francisco, CA

<u>The</u> <u>Case</u> <u>for</u> <u>Reincarnation</u>

<u>Wheels</u> <u>of</u> <u>Light:</u> <u>A</u> <u>Study</u> <u>of</u> <u>the</u> <u>Chakras</u> by Rosalyn L. Bruyere. 1991
    Bon Productions, Sierra Madre, California
    A riveting book. Don't miss it.

photo by Jon Nicholas

PART 2:

ACTION
- DO IT -

Now that you have an overview of your trip, it is time for action.

HYPNO-GRESSION • JOURNEY OF BREATH
VIBRATION • TOUCH • SOUND

Each road leads back to yourself. Happy trails to you.

Oh, how I love to go behind my eyes
spiraling into the black holes of fathomless brain cells;
swirling, never ending into lands with no name.
Shrines built of shrines.
Gardens lost to halls
timeless in time.

I journey the me behind my mind
tickled by fleeting glimpses:
A boy dancing naked and alone.
Animated wheat eating breakfast made of meat.
Jumping beans with Mexican hats.
A silver spoon.
A curled up cat.

Come with me a jumble dancing,
we'll slide and laugh and leave a-prancing.

CHAPTER 4

HYPNO-GRESSION:
TRANSFORMATIONAL TRAVEL

Close your eyes.
Focus your attention.
Recapture, remember
in Multi Dimension.

As a professional hypnotherapist, the hypno-therapeutic approach still remains my personal favorite mode of trance-portation. That is why I devote this separate chapter to the journey of self hypnosis. I have included a self hypnosis regression script that you might like to record in your own voice. When you play it you will become your own hypnosis guide, or you may order my recording of Time Travel: Do-It-Yourself Hypnosis.

This approach to inner journey is very popular with hypnotherapists. I have used it with hundreds of people and have had astounding results. There are five phases in a hypno-gression. They involve the INDUCTION PHASE, THE DEEPENING PHASE, THE JOURNEY PHASE, THE INTEGRATION PHASE AND THE "COME ON BACK" PHASE. In each phase I offer many options for you to choose and use in the "how to do it" instructions at the end of this chapter.

Hypno-gression in Detail: Options & Techniques

I BLESS MYSELF

> Bless me on all levels
> Physically, mentally
> Emotionally and spiritually
> So I may truly
> recognize and fulfill my life's purpose.
> Let all teachings be for the highest good
> of myself and humanity.
> Help me reconnect
> with my special gifts
> and let me lovingly shed any
> negative messages given by insensitive people.
>
> Thank you.
> Amen.

THE INDUCTION PHASE

The goal of the induction phase is to turn your focus inward. There are as many ways to induce altered consciousness as there are people in the universe. You may purposefully induce a hypno-gression or wait until one happens spontaneously during your daily mental rhythms. You decide. After you choose your favorite induction, use it for step 1 on page 37 "How To Do Your Own Hypno-gression".

Spontaneous Inductions

Trance-induction is so natural that you spontaneously go in and out of it throughout your day. You just don't call it hypnosis or trance. Utilize any of these natural inductions for your hypno-gression if you think that the time and place is appropriate.

- Upon awakening - when you are no longer asleep and not yet wide awake

- Just before you enter sleep state at night

- While experiencing a "runner's high" or "athlete's high"

- When making love

- When daydreaming

Voluntary Inductions

The following eleven inductions work beautifully to move you into inner focus. They are each powerful and fun. Choose the one you prefer.

1. Pleasant Scene Visualization
Close your eyes and take yourself to a pleasant scene in your imagination. Perhaps to a place you've really been. A place in your own backyard or a place that you've visited in a dream. Your favorite place might be a new spot created in this very moment in time.

2. Fractional Relaxation
In this technique, you (just like a droning teacher you may have had) bore, fatigue, and tire your conscious mind into taking a short vacation. One technique of fractional relaxation is to start at your toes. Think about each toe in detail. Tense your toes and relax them. Move your concentration to the ball of the foot, to the arch, and then to the heel of the foot. Tighten the foot and relax it. In the minutest detail, work your way up through your entire trunk, to your arms, your hands, around your skull and across your eyelids. Another technique is to count your breaths. With each inspiration, imagine white light. Hum softly the word "relax". If you are a visual person, use that sense. If you are auditory, use sounds. If you are kinesthetic, use sensations and feelings. Or, work with all of these. If you prefer, chart the journey of your body.

3. Counting Backwards
Count backwards from one through twenty, imagining yourself entering a place in your imagination with each count.

4. Gazing and Wondering
- Fix your gaze lightly on an object a few feet away.

- Silently talk to yourself about three things you see, three things you hear, and three things you feel. Then, talk to yourself about two things you see, things you hear, and two things you feel. Next, talk to yourself about one thing you see, thing you hear, and one thing you feel. Note, that if your eyes want to close, let them and go on

- As you go farther into a trance, begin to wonder which of your arms or hands will become lighter. Lift that arm or hand from the spot where it is resting with a true subconscious motion. Become aware of the curious sensations of wondering about such strange things. Notice the lifting or other movements and its directions. Wonder whether or how your hand will rise up and touch your face. When it does, will it return back to where it was resting? Or will the other hand rise up first?

- Continue to enjoy this pleasant, curious experience of subconscious motion

5. Out of Body

Lie on your back. Mentally float out of your body to a foot above yourself. Imagine you are suspended by strings and pulleys that pull you upward. As you float, become a detached observer and look carefully at your body, describing it in great detail and specificity. Cover your entire body slowly, describing everything you see and hear, commenting on areas of tension and comfort.

6. Track Your Thoughts

Become a witness, an objective observer to the thoughts you think. Observe your thoughts as they come and go. Notice how you, as the witness, can have your thoughts slow down or speed up. If you notice any unpleasant thoughts, simply open a door and let those thoughts leave. Invite pleasant, serene thoughts to take their place. Now, take a deep breath and become aware of the feeling of breathing. Hold the breath and when you let it go, take yourself even deeper into relaxation by saying "deeply relaxed".

7. Stare at a Pendulum

A popular induction technique is staring at a pendulum. You might try that as well. As you watch the repetitive swing from side to side, imagine you are the pendulum. Let yourself empathize and become the pendulum. Allow your body and breathing to feel the rhythm. Then, let your eyelids gently close down.

8. Non Dominant Hand

Take your non-dominant hand and hold it at eye level. Look at the back of your hand with your elbow slightly bent. Fix your eyes on a knuckle or index finger, keeping your fingers close together and very tight. The hand is going to move towards your face. This is normal. Your fingers will start to move apart as you move it towards your face. As this happens, close your eyes and enter a nice state of relaxation.

9. Blessings

Close your eyes and count on each of your blessing one by one, fully experiencing each one of them in detail. Take your time.

10. Meditate

Any way you like to meditate is fine.

11. Pray

Practice makes perfect! Whichever induction technique you choose, understand that the more often you practice the art of altered awareness, the easier it becomes.Each time your experience will be more wonderful than the one before. Relaxation becomes you.

DEEPENING THE TRANCE

Now that you have entered into a relaxed state of consciousness, it is time to deepen your trance. First, gauge how relaxed you are. Then you can gauge your relaxation. If you are a *visual* person imagine yourself pushing a measuring stick into soft earth and read the numbers on the measuring stick. The measure will tell you how deeply you are in trance. Then push it in deeper. If you are *tactile*, notice the amount of relaxation in your hands or the warmth of your body and increase those feelings. *Auditory?* You can tell the depth of your trance by the sound of your breathing slowing down.

Now, choose to move to an even deeper level. Tell yourself: "Take a few deep breaths and you will be five times more relaxed." Then take a deep breath. Hold it in and when you let it out, say: "Deeper, deeper, all the way down." Repeat this breath technique 5 times.

THE JOURNEY: GETTING THE MESSAGE

Say to yourself "I am going back now in time. Back into a past life." As the images or experiences manifest, notice what surfaces. Say them out loud so you may tape record them or if you have a sitter, they may scribe for you.

ASK YOUR "HAPPY ENDING" QUESTIONS   *(page 16 for more details)*

- **Feet?**   Look at your feet. This will ground you. Describe what you see
                     Notice if you have shoes.

- **Clothes?**   Notice what you are wearing or not wearing.

- **Senses?**   One by one, allow your experience to enter each of your
                     senses. Notice any smells, tastes, sounds, bodily
                     sensations, sights and extra sensory sensations.

- **Others?**   Are you alone or with someone?

- **Location?**   Are you inside or outside?

- **Time?**   What is the time period or year? What season is it?

- **Experience?**   What is happening? What happens next?

- **Death?**   Answer the question: "How did this entity die?"

- **•White Light**   Send that entity white light. Picture and imagine a flood of white light upon them and see what happens.

- **• Learned?**   "What have I learned from this lifetime" or "What message is this entity wishing to give me?"

INTEGRATION PHASE

Draw a mandala. Write down your experiences. Answer your ten questions on paper. Dance or move.

"COME ON BACK" PHASE

Get grounded by taking a vinegar bath. Give yourself some time to be with yourself.

HOW TO DO YOUR OWN HYPNO-GRESSION: STEP BY STEP

Before you begin, choose any one of the following three hypno-gression processes:

1. Listen to the cassette tape <u>Time</u> <u>Travel.</u>
   To order the tape see the order form at the end of this book.

2. Make <u>your own cassette</u> tape (a sample script is found on page 41)

3. Use the following step by step process:

I BLESS MYSELF

> Bless me on all levels
> Physically, mentally
> Emotionally and spiritually
> So I may truly
> recognize and fulfill my life's purpose.
> Let all teachings be for the highest good
> of myself and humanity.
> Help me reconnect
> with my special gifts
> and let me lovingly shed any
> negative messages given by insensitive people.
>
> Thank you.
> Amen.

MUSIC
   Put on some nice background music. Avoid music with lyrics, they can distract you.
   Turn on your tape recorder to record your session.

USE YOUR CHOSEN INDUCTION
   (Select one of the many that mentioned on page 32 or use one of your own.)

DEEPEN THE TRANCE
   (Techniques on page 35)

BEGIN YOUR JOURNEY

Go back (or forward in time) and be sure to complete these three important steps before your journey ends.

GATHER INFORMATION

• Answer the question: "How did this entity die?"

• Send that entity white light. Picture and imagine a flood of white light upon them and see what happens.

• Answer the question: "What have I learned from this lifetime?" or "What message is this entity wishing to give me?"

COME ON BACK

Count from 1 to 5, saying to yourself that at the count of 5 you will be alert, clear minded, and remember everything.

EXAMPLES OF HYPNO-GRESSION:
(USING THE "OUT OF BODY" INDUCTION)

Mud Man - Peru

Mud. I'm having a good time with mud. A place I know in Peru playing with mud, doing art - carving mud with sticks. I don't have to do anything else - carve mud. My carvings dry in the sun. I'm a funny fellow - a round face and rosy cheeks - I make people laugh. I make mud pies. Carving, I sit by the aqueduct, the mud cracks on my hands and fingers. I am a happy fellow. One old lady makes me unhappy. She lives in the village and hits me with sticks. I have to show her humility. She's important. She belongs in the priest house. I want to make mud and laughter and play. That's why she hits me with sticks.

I always have food. It's gruel. I always have friends. "Tucari". Tucari rubs my back. He has a round face like mine and broken teeth and old sandals. He sits with me when I do mud. He brings me gruel. He's an old friend.

The one with the red lips, she always comes and brings me flowers. Old people come and laugh and joke with me. Little boy comes - no little girls to talk to. The got taken away for the priestery. People here believe in virgin girls. Little baby girls are tied on their mother's backs before they get to be little girls and are taken away. Taken to the higher mountains to the priestery. This is a very old land - very old traditions. Sometimes old traditions stop making sense.

My body is solid with round belly, my arms get tired from the mud. My butt hurts, can't wipe myself too well. I have hot sores on my neck. I like this body. I like to make mud - I can't make mud anymore. I live in the house now made of mud with the mud decorations outside. Tucari Is there - the old woman (the mean Old woman) died. I was glad; I wanted her to die after she died. I hated her. I always knew she'd go away. I waited her out and I'm glad. I hated being alive with her. Now she is dead.

My legs have sores all over them. Tucari talks a lot. Tells a lot of stories about fighting. He fought once. Fought invaders before he came here. He's proud of that. He thinks he's a warrior. I do, too. He doesn't smell too good. He needs to go down to the river. He smells like dying or maybe it's me. My legs have sores all over. The sores will eat me into dying. I've seen them before, ate others into dying. I'll be eaten into dying too. I had a nice time with the mud. Learned patience - I didn't learn humility. I couldn't to it because of that old lady. I learned joy - simple joy. It was a good one - I didn't learn humility because of that hag. I waited her out and didn't learn it. (I'm not finished with her. It's my mother. Yah.)

They dug a ditch and put me in it. Flowers on me. People cried. My soul didn't leave my body until the night. It left through my heart. Tucari's in the house. I said goodbye to him. He cried. I'm at peace.

Bride   (Using the "track your thoughts" inductions)

I see a bride in a long train. She is getting married. Little round black flowers in her hair. Funny black hat with red trim. She's getting married to Silbe. Her name is Kresha. She is going to get married. They play musical instruments like the snake charmer and chant. It is the third day of the wedding. Silbe's uncle is very rich and important. Krishna. A big temple blesses the wedding. Krishna. It is held in the building with round spires. (It looks like the soft serve ice cream cone.) They "hoo, hoo, hoo". She wears the little black satin shoes her uncle gave her.

They shave the hair from her femaleness. Tonight they will check sheets for blood. She is very nervous. 13 years old. He has dark skin. The color of mango skin.

Tonight they will eat sweet rice and drink blood from the sheep. Her long braids are wrapped and twisted behind her head. There are many flowers and much incense. She is tired from the "hoo, hoo, hoo" and music of snake charmers. She must not sleep or be afraid. She was born of the right family. They will go to the large city, the city with the Ali. It is a large mosque. It was built for his beautiful queen. Ali. Alibabra. Alibabra. They say that she still lives in the roofs of the mosques and that she blesses the people. And we will live in the big city. The marketplace stretched with course brown fabrics the color of Earth. They will sell semsi (round and orange), roachi (yellow, white, orange grain. Very good. Must soak it first) and dargra (comes from animal, looks like bacon)

I do not know how to cook. I do not cook but I will learn. I like honey. I like the candy made with honey and the dough dripping with honey. Father says not to eat too much but it is good. I like the nuts and honey: It runs down my chin and fingers. It is very good. I like father, he is nice. We are a good family. The right family. (chants)

I am a servant of my family, of my father, of his house. And now I will be a servant to the family of my husband. I'm scared but I can't tell anyone. I'm tired. This wedding takes a long time. Only men and me in the mosque.

My God. They have pulled my skirt up. He is sticking his penis in me. All are watching. It is awful. They are yelling and cheering. I'm bleeding. It hurts me. Laughing and chanting. Oh no, this is terrible. I feel so ashamed. So ashamed. Did this happen to my mother too? Why didn't anyone tell me. I will bring shame to my father's house. My husband is my master now. I must conquer my feelings. I am a servant now to my husband. I will never forget this day and I will never talk of this day. It is a terrible day. It hurts much.

She had 5 children. She lived in a very large house near the mosque. She grew very fat. Her husband was a good husband. Lots of food. Lots of servants. Lots of children. She never forgot that day. He broke her womanhood and he broke her heart. She died of a cough. A bad cough. She was very fat. Fat in the hips and belly. 64. She died with two children stroking her. She died with honey nut candy beside her. She died happy.

I send her the light and she leaves through her heart and she flies like wings.

I learned patience and forgiveness.

A Visit from my Deceased Mother
(My mother died in 1986. I had this encounter with her in 1990 using the "out of body" induction.)

My left arm is cold. I see the body lying on the floor. Arm over the face. The left arm is cold. I see Sandra (my guide) sitting on the sofa. I see the tape going around on the player.

I see my lipstick almost worn off. My lips look dry. I see a lady with white hair. Pure white hair. (It is my mother.) "Hello dear" she says. "How are you?" "I've been very busy. If you think it is busy on earth, wait until you get to heaven. I'm funnier than ever. I tell jokes all the time." I go to the movie studios and try for an audition. My life was my youth. My life was the day I got out of my house. Out of New York. Out of the drugstore. Out of the phone booth in the drugstore. Out of the phone booth where boyfriends would call me. I had beautiful fingernails, beautiful hats, beautiful clothes. I had a fur collar. I was in style.

HYPNO-GRESSION SCRIPT

Here is a sample script you may record in your own voice and play for yourself as you journey within. When the script asks a question, leave a quiet space so you may process your answer during your trance. This hypno-gression script has been adapted from the late Helen Wambach's brilliant research.

INSTRUCTIONS: Find a place where you can relax without being disturbed for 15 to 20 minutes. Get comfortable. Stretch out comfortably on your back, with your feet 8 to 10 inches apart. Loosen any tight fitting apparel which may bother you. You may play soft music.

INDUCTION

I become aware of the feeling and sensations of my body. I become aware of the feeling of my body as it rests upon the surface where I am lying or sitting. I become aware of my breathing. I track my breathing. I notice air going in and out of my lungs. It is as if I am fully in my body and yet at the same time I have flashes of knowing that I am more than my body; more than my breathing; more than my heart beating. I let my mind drift off to pleasant scenes in my imagination. Now, I will think about a time when I was tired (perhaps sitting in front of a fire) and I just dozed off to sleep. I picture, in my mind, that scene and remember when I began to breathe deeply and fully. I feel my breathing. I experience breathing slowing down, deeply and fully.

DEEPENING

I give myself permission to take a deep breath. After I take a breath, I hold it in for as long as I'm comfortable. When I let it out, I let myself go even deeper down, ten times more relaxed than before. As I let the air out, I say: "deeper and deeper". Now, I take a second breath using the same technique. Now, I take a third breath.

THE JOURNEY

All discomfort I greet with the words 'calm and relaxed' and my muscles relax. My body is deeply relaxed and my mind is unusually alert and I have easy access to my memories. I don't think, analyze or interpret. I go back into my memory and find a photograph of myself that was taken between the ages of thirteen and eighteen. I will focus on just one snapshot.

Back in time, I notice what I am wearing. Look closely. Do I like my outfit? Notice how it feels on my body? I look down at my feet and see my shoes. If I am not sure what they look like, I make up a story.

Back into my memory, I find a picture of myself taken between the ages of six and twelve. As I look closely at that picture, I notice where I am when the picture is taken. Remembering more and more details of that place where the picture is taken.

I am back now in the fourth grade. I am sitting in class, in my regular seat in the fourth grade". Are the windows on my left, or on my right? Is there gum under the desk? The teacher is in the front of the room. I want to ask her a question and her name flashes into my memory.

Back in my memory I find a picture of myself taken between the ages of one and five. Look into the eyes of that child who is you and let yourself be three. I remember being in my small body sitting in my bathtub. I am vividly aware of my body. I look down and see my thighs, my knees, my legs, my ankles, my feet and toes. I notice how it feels to be in my small body.

Now, line up all three snapshots. Myself as a young child, myself in middle-childhood, myself as a teen. What is it that has stayed the same? My body changed, my clothing changed, and the background of the pictures have changed. What remains me?

Each snapshot represents just one twentieth of a second of the time I have been alive in this lifetime. If those 1/20th of a seconds were placed in a row behind the picture of myself as a young child, these snapshots would stretch to infinity. Behind the picture of myself in middle-childhood, again the row of snapshots stretches with all the other one-twentieths of a second that I experienced in my growing-up years. And that row stretches to infinity. Behind the row of myself as an adolescent, stretches the row of the other one-twentieths of a second that you lived through during that period of my life. If all the changes of my body as I matured sexually were recorded on film, if all the changes in my feelings, my ambitions, my dreams had been caught by a camera, they too would stretch to infinity.

As I look back now on these endless rows that represent my past until the age of eighteen, I understand that much of the past I remember is a story told to me by my conscious mind, which remembers fragments and pieces from the past and threads them together to make a story called, 'My Past,' much as a film editor strings together snippets from film to make a movie. The past I think I remember is fragmentary and limited. For every moment in my past when I think I hated someone, I can find a moment when I loved that person. For every moment in my past where I felt guilt and shame, is a moment I felt triumph and quiet self-satisfaction. Lost in those endless rows of snapshots of my growing-up years are potentials that are yet to be developed, feelings I have long since forgotten, options I haven't yet realized. At this moment, my past is nearly as changeable as my future. I may choose to remember parts of my past life, since forgotten, and I may choose to realize their potential in a future that is also mine to choose. This is what is meant by free will.

My body is lying heavy on the floor, deeply relaxed. My body is so heavy it feels as though it's sinking very gently onto the floor. My mind is free and light, floating, alert, deeply comfortable and relaxed. It is as if I am a pinpoint of consciousness floating up away from your body and hovering near the ceiling of this room. I am looking down now from the ceiling of this room.

I am floating out through the roof of this building and a mist out into the clear air. (The stars are sparkling bright and the moon is out, and below you the city lies covered with snow.) I float higher and higher, up into the velvety blackness of space. I feel marvelously light and free as I soar up and away.

I speak now to my subconscious mind and reduce my brain wave electrical potentials down to five cycles per second. My brain wave amplitude readings will be five cycles per second. At this deep, slow-wave state, I reach the deeper portions of myself where answers live. As I count to five, my brain wave activity slows to five cycles per second. One, deeper and deeper. Two, more and more relaxed. Three. Four. Five.

GATHERING INFORMATION

- Go now to the time just before my birth into my current lifetime. Am I choosing to be born? *(Pause)*

- Does anyone help me choose? *(Pause)* If anyone helps me choose, what is my relationship to the counselor? *(Pause)*

- How do I feel about the prospect of living this coming lifetime? *(Pause)*

- Am I choosing the last half of the twentieth century to experience physical life for a reason? What is that reason? *(Pause)*

- Have I chosen my sex for this lifetime? If I have, why have I chosen to focus as a man or a woman in this lifetime? *(Pause)*

- What is my purpose for coming into my current lifetime? *(Pause)*

- I direct my attention to my mother-to-be. Have I known her in a past life? If I have known her, what was our relationship before? *(Pause)*

- I direct my attention to my father-to-be. Have I known him in a past life? If so, what was our relationship before? *(Pause)*

- Am I aware now, before being born, of others that I will know in this coming lifetime? Have I known them in past lifetimes? Do I know what role they will play in my coming life? Will I know them as lovers, or mates? Will I know them as children or other relatives? Will I know them as friends? *(Pause)*

- I direct my attention to the developing fetus who will be me. Am I experiencing myself inside the fetus? Outside the fetus? In and out? When does my consciousness fully join that of the fetus? *(Pause)*

- I notice the attitudes and feelings of my mother just prior to my birth. *(Pause)*

- As I move down the birth canal I will have no pain, yet I will be aware of all sensations. As I move down the birth canal, I notice my experiences. *(Long Pause)*

- Now I emerge from the birth canal. I am born! I notice what that is like for me. *(Long Pause)*

- What are the attitudes and feelings of others in the delivery room after my birth? *(Pause)*

Now I leave that place...floating up and away from the delivery room, floating back up into space, back up to my cloud. I climb onto my cloud, and stretch out and relax, any awareness of pain and discomfort leaves me. As I float on my cloud, and as I count, all my body systems return to normal. I have no physical or emotional discomfort as a result of my experiences on this trip. I float up and away from that place where I was born. My body is relaxed and all my organ systems are returning to a healthy normal state. As I float on my cloud, I go deeper. As I count I become more and more peaceful and serene. My mind is floating free, and I have a feeling of peace and harmony around me. Five, deeper and deeper. Four, more and more relaxed. Three. Two. One. On my cloud there is a beautiful white light all around me. The light is pure and intense, growing brighter. There is a tightly budded blossom in my solar plexus. Rays of energy from the light gently unfurl the petals until the heart are exposed. Dancing rays of energy from the light flood into the heart of the blossom, and move through my solar plexus. The energy waves from the light cleanses any negative after-effects from my experience on this trip. The waves of light energy bring a lightness, peace, and serenity to my mind and my body.

COME ON BACK

It is time now to return to the here and now. When I awaken, the answers that flashed in my mind will be vivid in my memory. They will remain vivid for months and I will be able to recall them whenever I wish. When I return to my present awareness, I will write down my answers easily.

Imagine now a ball of golden energy sparkling out of a far corner of space. I Picture that energy rolling and flowing down through the darkness of space, penetrating the atmospheric envelope of earth, coming down to this room and entering the crown of my head. As the energy enters the crown of my head, a sense of well-being sweeps through me, and all my bodily energies are renewed. As I return to my social awareness, I feel great. One, the ball of energy is moving now into the crown of my head and into my face. Two, the ball of energy is moving into my jaw muscles and into my neck. Three, the energy is moving into my shoulders down my wrists, hands and fingers. Five, the energy is moving from my shoulders down my torso to my waist. Six, the energy is moving into my hips. Seven, the energy is flowing down my thighs. Eight, the energy is moving down my legs, ankles, feet, and toes. Nine, my body is alive now with vibrant energy and I'm ready to return, feeling refreshed, feeling great. Ten, I open my eyes, awake, feeling great and I stretch.

RESOURCE LIST

Do-It-Yourself Hypnosis Cassette tape by Shelley Lessin Stockwell.
    Creativity Unlimited Press, 30819 Casilina, Rancho Palos Verdes, CA 90274

Do-It-Yourself Hypnosis Workbook by Shelley Lessin Stockwell.
    Creativity Unlimited Press, 30819 Casilina, Rancho Palos Verdes, CA 90274

Smile on Your Face, Money in Your Pocket: Do-It-Yourself Hypnosis
    by Shelley Lessin Stockwell.
    Creativity Unlimited Press, 30819 Casilina, Rancho Palos Verdes, CA 90274.

Reframing by Bandler and Grinder; 1982; Real People Press

Hypnosis for Change by Hadley and Staudacher; New York; Ballantine Books

Life Before Life ; by Helen Wambach; 1979; New York; Bantam Books.

Photo by Dennis Briskin

CHAPTER 5

INSPIRATION:
THE JOURNEY OF BREATH
(REBIRTHING AND HOLOTROPIC BREATHING)

I breathe golden sunset.
Kaleidoscope wonder.
I am the sunset..

REBIRTHING

"Fathers help but mothers deliver." -Diane Zimberoff

Rebirthing is a gentle form of breathwork used as a regression technique. Leonard Orr and Sondra Ray have done much to popularize this approach to the subconscious (superconscious) mind. The first phase or "induction" part of the process involves a circular breathing technique followed by inner focus.

Some people fear that deep breathing will cause oxygen deprivation or hyperventilation. The following techniques do quite the opposite: they give you extra oxygen. These "super" ventilation styles use full deep and relaxed exhalations. Hyperventilation is caused by shallow panting exhalations which stops the oxygen flow. I have never understood why certain actual birth preparation techniques require limited panting breaths just when mom and baby need oxygen the most!

My versions of rebirthing can be done in 2 styles, the loose approach or a more structured plan. Each are powerful. Try them both and chose your favorite.

IF YOU ARE ASSISTING A BREATHER

If you are assisting a breather, clear your mind, relax and envision a loving, positive session. Stay in your integrity and be lovingly detached.

Some assistants read the instructions out loud to the breather.

You might run your hands about 5" above the breather feeling their energy (aura). If your hands tingle or get very hot or cold above a chakra ask "what is going on here?"

Feel the aura (energy around the breather). Allow your instincts to intuit any physical blocks, i.e. let's say the breather tightens his forehead. Go ahead and touch the forehead asking: "What is going on here?"

THE LOOSE APPROACH – HOW TO DO IT

I BLESS MYSELF

> Bless me on all levels
> Physically, mentally
> Emotionally and spiritually
> So I may truly
> recognize and fulfill my life's purpose.
> Let all teachings be for the highest good
> of myself and humanity.
> Help me reconnect
> with my special gifts
> and let me lovingly shed any
> negative messages given by insensitive people.
>
> Thank you.
> Amen.

MUSIC
Nice music, if you like.

BREATH IN A CIRCLE
Use deep connected relaxed breaths. Link each full-lung inspiration (inhalation) to each cleansing breath (exhalation) without any pauses. Let your breath be easy and relaxed. Choose to breathe either through your nose or through your mouth. Make sure both your in and out breaths are done through the mouth (my preference) or the nose. Never in one and out the other.

KEEP BREATHING

Keep breathing for at least 10 minutes. Don't quit. Let your breath weave into the music. Imagine that the breath is breathing you. Experience whatever comes up. As with all enlightenment techniques, do not think, analyze, or judge this material. Just let it be. If the images are scary...keep breathing. If you experience bodily sensations or tightness...keep breathing. No matter what, keep it up until you experience a feeling of surrender, ecstasy, or as the scientist call it...integration.

LET IT HAPPEN

Express any feelings and release energy by kicking your feet, moving your head from side to side, letting out sounds or words, hitting a pillow with your fists or a bataka (cloth bat) or a rubber pipe. Let out any sound that wants to emerge.

GETTING THE MESSAGE

- **Feet?** Look at your feet. This will ground you. Describe what you see Notice if you have shoes.

- **Clothes?** Notice what you are wearing or not wearing.

- **Senses?** One by one, allow your experience to enter each of your senses. Notice any smells, tastes, sounds, bodily sensations,sights and extra sensory sensations.

- **Others?** Are you alone or with someone?

- **Location?** Are you inside or outside?

- **Time?** What is the time period or year? What season is it?

- **Experience?** What is happening? What happens next?

- **Death?** Answer the question: "How did this entity die?"

- **White Light** Send that entity white light. Picture and imagine a flood of white light upon them and see what happens.

- **Learned?** "What have I learned from this lifetime" or "What message is this entity wishing to give me?"

COMING TO A CLOSE

How do you know when you are done? You will know. There will be release and peace. It's like knowing when an orgasm is done. You know.

WELCOME BACK

Draw a mandala. Write down your experiences. Take a walk. In general, ground yourself.

EXAMPLE USING REBIRTHING TECHNIQUE: THE LOOSE APPROACH

Harem Girl

I have a veil over my nose. I am hidden. A harem girl. I am a harem girl. I dance. I'm too skinny to be a harem girl, but I dance anyway. I try to get fat but I can't. I'm not hungry and the other girls try to feed me. Not hungry enough.

Eight girls - "Sylvie", "Gloria" (her name's not Gloria but its Gloria), "Munchee". A guy's in the harem - a eunuch - he's there to take care of us. Protect us, "Gregory". He has a hearing problem. Doesn't hear very well.

I like to dance - please the master and his friends. They always laugh 'cause I am so skinny. I'm skinny when all others are fat. I like to make love with master. He likes to make love with me, too. We make love lots and lots. They always try to make me fat. Master says when he makes me fat with baby, I'll be fatter. He has a beard, a big beard, a big long beard, blue eyes with one brown spot in one. One eye is very blue - he is blind in that eye.

Bugs brought blindness. I have beautiful, black eyes. Shiny eyes. Master smells good. Master born to family where he is master to harem. He lets me be master when we make love. Smiles when he sees me. He has pretty teeth. He has many camels. Many friends, much food. Many harem girls. He likes women best. He lounges in the middle and we all cuddle him. He is a good man. An honorable man.

I like to dance. I can't get fatter, I don't know why.

I'm older, I got fatter. I was his favorite. I run the whole house now. He spends most of his time with me. He's getting very old now. We are good friends. I love him. He loves me. We are all his wives. He dies before me. I am very sad I want to go with him now. I will will myself to go with him. I will stop eating. Funny, I always wanted to be fatter. I will die skinny. Will die with my master. My heart is broken. I will die of a broken heart. I will die because my heart is broken. I will talk to no one.

She died of a broken heart. It took her a long time to die. She was in great pain. She spoke to no one; not even the eunuch. He stood by her bedside. The others didn't understand. She was happy and solid and a little too skinny. (He was Steve from Shelley's lifetime) I learned love - real love. And devotion - conviction. A good one. He loved, he was the teacher. I was very young. He was very wise and a good human. I was loyal and devoted and joyous and trusting and loving. It was a really good life time. I'm proud of it. I haven't changed much from that one. I learned the lessons well. I know how to love from then. The ape didn't know how to love that's why I had that one. Mainly the loving. That's my specialty.

Ape

I'm an ape - a big ape - one of the biggest there is. I pound my chest. Bigger than the rest. I am a big ape and I sing. I sing ape songs better than any other ape.

I have a territory and nobody comes in my territory unless I let them. I am powerful. I make little apes. I f—— lady apes. I have lots of apes. I create apes. I am chief of all the apes, nobody messes with me.

I swing in the trees. I carry around little apes. I have other apes pick me. I eat any time I want to - I bare my teeth. I'm a mean ape - I like it - nobody messes with me 'cause I kill them.

When I was a little ape someone killed my mother. Nobody messes with me again. I'm one mean ape - I make little apes. Ain't gonna be a little ape without a mom or me in my territory, I'm the meanest God damn ape in the world. I like it. I do exactly what I want to do.

(My sitter, Barbara, asks - How did you die?)

I fell off a branch and got impaled on another one. I was old. No one ever messes with me. My arms are tired from the trees.

THE STRUCTURED APPROACH – HOW TO DO IT:

CHOOSE YOUR COURSE

Choose what you want to explore. A physical pain? It might be a feeling (ie: I feel unhappy all the time) and allow yourself to let go into that feeling, seeing where it take you. A limiting attitude or behavior? ("Everyone is always on my back") Choose a sentence or phrase to best identify that limiting attitude or pain.

MUSIC

Put on some nice, soothing music.

BREATHE IN A CIRCLE

Use deep connected relaxed breaths. Link each full-lung inspiration (inhalation) to each cleansing breath (exhalation) without any pauses. Let your breath be easy and relaxed. Choose to breathe either through your nose or through your mouth. Make sure both your in and out breaths are done through the mouth (my preference) or the nose. Never in one and out the other.

I BLESS MYSELF

> Bless me on all levels
> Physically, mentally
> Emotionally and spiritually
> So I may truly
> recognize and fulfill my life's purpose.
> Let all teachings be for the highest good
> of myself and humanity.
> Help me reconnect
> with my special gifts
> and let me lovingly shed any
> negative messages given by insensitive people.
>
> Thank you.
> Amen.

KEEP BREATHING

Keep breathing! Experience whatever comes up. As with enlightenment techniques, do not think, analyze or judge this material. Just let it be. If the images are scary ...keep breathing. If you experience bodily sensations or tightness...keep breathing. No matter what, keep it up until you experience a feeling of surrender, ecstasy, or as the scientist call it...integration.

LET IT HAPPEN

Express any feelings and release energy by kicking your feet, moving your head from side to side, letting out sounds or words, hitting a pillow with your fists, a bataka (cloth bat) or a rubber pipe. Let out any sound that emerges. Don't hold back.

ASK YOUR QUESTIONS

• Feet?	Look at your feet. This will ground you. Describe what you see Notice if you have shoes.
• Clothes?	Notice what you are wearing or not wearing.
• Senses?	One by one, allow your experience to enter each of your senses. Notice any smells, tastes, sounds, bodily sensations,sights and extra sensory sensations.
• Others?	Are you alone or with someone?
• Location?	Are you inside or outside?
• Time?	What is the time period or year? What season is it?
• Experience?	What is happening? What happens next?
• Death?	Answer the question: "How did this entity die?"
• White Light	Send that entity white light. Picture and imagine a flood of white light upon them and see what happens.
• Learned?	"What have I learned from this lifetime" or "What message is this entity wishing to give me?"

COMING TO A CLOSE

How do you know when you are done? You will know. There will be release and peace. It's like knowing when an orgasm is done. You know.

WELCOME BACK

Draw a mandala. Write down your experiences. Take a walk. In general, ground yourself.

EXAMPLE USING REBIRTHING : THE STRUCTURED APPROACH
(Rebirthing Regression guided by Diane Zimberoff)

Before this regression, I had chosen to explore a vague irrational fear I had of dying. I also wanted to understand my strong sugar cravings. As I breathed, I reported my feelings as they came through. I noticed my jaw was tight. What was I holding back? I reported my feelings. An onlooker reported the experience like this: "She began to talk in an old woman's voice as if she had no teeth. She said she hated cooking and breathing all the smoke inside the "round place" covered in skins. She wanted to be outside with the others, with the children.

She began hitting the ground with the hose, said she had arthritis in her hands and legs, couldn't hit hard. Said she was hitting with the big spoon, getting food all over. Said Big Bear died and she wants to die too, but they would not let her."

This session was videotaped. Here are the transcripts:

Old Squaw

(Deep Breathing) "I have to make lots of food. Not enough food for everybody. Not enough food for me. I don't have enough to eat. I'm hungry. I look fat but I'm not, I'm hungry. I have to cook all this food and I can't eat. I don't have any teeth. I don't know why, they all fell out.

(Putting the feelings in motion I tried to kick my feet) "Not enough. I'm hungry. I need more. I don't have any teeth. I can't eat. I am very old lady. I am starving to death. I can't kick arthritis in my legs."

"They always leave me here to cook. That makes me angry. This is a round place. Got skins over the roof. Have to breathe this smoke. I don't like it. They all get to go out and be with the children and the animals and I have to be here and cook. It really makes me mad!" (Using a rubber hose, I hit the floor to release new energy) "Food all over. My spoon it will break. So angry. Big Bear will be mad. Big Bear died. I have arthritis. I'm hungry. I want to eat something. Arthritis in my hands and legs came when my teeth fell out. I must stir the pot of corn and venison." (my guide, Diane asks "Where did the arthritis come from?") "Big Bear died. I died too but I can't die now. I have to cook the food. They won't let me die. He got to die but not me. (I let out a large sigh and relaxed which is generally the sign of a reliving phase of a regression) "Poor lady: she wasn't very bright."

I then went on to recall in vivid detail my own birth, my feelings of disappointment of being removed from my mother, and most importantly, my feelings of being debilitated by my mother's taking drugs during the pregnancy and at the birth. When my mother took drugs, so did I. I felt paralyzed. I felt like I was dead. My first bonding with my mother came the next day after my birth and my mother held me lovingly and fed me very sweet drink that tasted exactly like the candy I have craved ever since.

Massai

I kill animals - I am Massai - I kill animals. I kill animals for fun and food. I am considered very good at killing animals. I will kill any animal. I used to kill birds for fun. I can kill any animal. One time I killed a boy - for fun. Just wanted to see what it was like. It was fun. Like killing an animal. No big deal. I won't do it again. It made lots of trouble. His family was very angry. I slit his neck. He was eight; from the stick village. His family did nothing. It is very hot here. Many bugs.

(What did you do after you slit his throat?)
I cried - but don't tell anyone - I didn't know him, I just wanted to see what it was like - no one must know I cried. I kill animals. I am famous for killing animals. I am very brave and strong and tall. Very black, very powerful. I must never cry.

(Who do you love?)
I love that boy - later. I love my sharp stick. I love my long legs.

(Why did you love the boy later?)
He spoke to me later - not in words - he said "I forgive you."

I am very strong. I can't be wrong. My power will leave. Power comes from locking my mind. I must think like a warrior., a hunter. People would laugh. I am really a hunter. I bring food, feed clothes - feed many, better than anyone else, I am the best hunter. That is my job. That is who you are. That is who I am. I must keep my mind strong, like my legs. My legs are like antelope - Swift.

(Do you have other powers?)
I have power in my balls, in my penis. I don't know where my power comes from.

(Is there power besides yours?)
No, not really.

(What makes the sun shine? Do you?)
SHUT UP.

HOLOTROPIC BREATHING

"Holotropic" (moving toward wholeness) is the name of a personal growth exploration style created by Stan and Christina Grof. As a scholar-in-residence at Esalan Institute in Big Sur, CA, Grof wanted to recreate the enlightenment experiences that he had recorded during 25 years of LSD research.

All of his subjects, whether healthy, psychiatric patients, terminally ill, or criminals, reported almost identical experiences. They accessed and resolved inner conflicts and reported feeling deeply healed and more peaceful. Many described it as a spiritual rebirthing process. Stan and Christina found that breathing deeply to provocative music paralleled the LSD enlightenment studies. Oxygen released the nervous system into a powerful spiritual emotional awakening (or reawakening perhaps). Thus, holotropic breathwork was born!

To do this process, you breathe fully and rapidly to provocative music. A Grof breath worker or friend may assist you as a sitter giving you any comforting touch or handholding or you may choose to take the Shelley style of singular journey.

HOW TO DO IT

MUSIC
To take this style of breath journey on your own, put on "provocative", stirring music, chanting or rhythms. Make sure that the music is long enough to last the time you choose for your experience and that it ends on a peaceful note. A breathwork session can be 15 minutes to 3 hours long. For your first session, I recommend 60 minutes followed by a 1 1/2 hour journey the next day. Of course if something starts happening, keep going.

BREATHING
The breathing is more rapid and deeper than normal breathing. I prefer to do it in through the nostrils and out through the mouth but you decide how you would like to do it. It is very important that the breathing remain full, as though you were breathing down to the tips of your toes, full deep breaths in. Full cleansing breaths out, rapidly, one right after the other. Ask your sitter (if you have one) to encourage this full and rapid breathing. Think of it as a deep internal bath of oxygen. Occasionally people experience a feeling like bands around their foreheads, at their wrists or ankles. A few people might experience an uncomfortable "heady" feeling. Just keep breathing. These feelings will deepen, give you information and evaporate into the oxygen and the music, opening and cleansing you.

VISIONS

As you are breathing, unresolved sequences from childhood may emerge. You might confront death or birth. And, of course, you may access visions and experiences from other places and other times. (In Stan Grof's words "Anything biographical, parental, or transpersonal may emerge.")

There are no rights or wrongs in this or any of our processes. Each person can experience things through images or physical sensations, through any of their senses. The results, however, are always the same - a wonderful feeling of awareness and clarity about your life and your life's purpose. Respect whatever comes up: it is your process for <u>now</u>.

BIRTH PHASES AND LIFE DECISIONS

An interesting aspect of this kind of breathing is Stan's theory of birth phases. While breathing you might re-live the phases of your own birth. The one particular phase that makes the biggest imprint or impression upon you could determine the rest of your now life. Stan sees birth as having four distinct phases. The decisions you made at birth, according to Stan, often become the blueprint of your life attitude.the meaning of your life, be they positive or negative, he believes, are aligned to the phase where you place the most energy. His four phases are:

PHASE OF BIRTH	LIFE ATTITUDES
Floating in the Womb with room	+ Complete relaxation, mellow bliss
Crammed in the womb-No Exit	+ Feeling your limits – Sad, helpless, hopeless
Labor	+ Strive to succeed and cooperating, – Life is a struggle, rage
Delivery	+ Win success ecstacy,intense joy, – – Unloved, lonely, hurt

EXAMPLE USING HOLOTROPIC BREATHING

Twins

When I was 33 years old I became pregnant and was elated. Four months into a queasy pregnancy, I began "spotting" and apparently was experiencing a miscarriage. I was sent for ultrasound testing. The ultrasound technician said "I see a septum separating the egg sac and two little fetuses deteriorating. Shelley, you miscarried twins." I was very upset and decided to go up to Esalan Institute in Big Sur, California before I was required to return to my job as a TWA flight attendant. I called Esalan and what classes they were offering next week. They gave me a list of classes including one called "Death and rebirth". I signed up for "Death and rebirth" with Stan and Christina Grof. During the course of the week, I learned about holotropic breathing and during an hour to two hour breathwork session, I had the following experience. Since this was a nonverbal experience, it is a little difficult to share it in words but I will do the best I can.

I felt bands of pressure around my forehead and wrists. The pressure mounted. Then suddenly it was as if I had burst through into another world, more magnificent, stunning, and glorious than anything I had ever heard or read about. I was flying upward to an orb of white light. My flying was done by a sensation behind each of my "wing bones". As I moved upward toward the orb, I felt an unknown level of ecstasy. Imagine the biggest orgasm of your life multiplied by 100. That is how it felt.

Up, up I flew moving toward that brilliant orb of light. I felt detached from my physical body except for an occasional feeling or sensation of someone gently sliding me sideways. I was told later that I was sliding across the floor and that my hands were floating upward.

I saw a ring of white garbed "souls" holding hands in a large circle as I ascended. They were magnificent. Each radiating peace and beauty. They were neither male nor female. Radiant light beings I didn't know. All I knew, in those moments without words, were that these white robed visions were all of mankind. Loving and peaceful. I rose above them, flying in my ecstasy and then I saw her. The wisest most knowing of all. I had to smile and a thought came to me at that moment. The "all knowing" was a woman who looked like the Statue of Liberty. I flew about her swooning in the rapture. After some time or else a year (you totally lose track of all time when you are in this consciousness) I had my second thought. "What about the twins?" I extended my right hand and magically there was a small person on it. I extended my left hand and another small person alighted. I flew, giddy and joyous, with my two small friends who suddenly grew larger and larger. They flew to me and one extended their hand and the other extended their hand below and together they lifted me upon their hands and flew me into forever. Bliss.

My awareness was that my miscarriage was no accident but a perfectly timed and planned step to bring me here to learn techniques and to open the door to my spirituality, enlightenment, and understanding. In the hours after this experience I had a strong desire to sit in the sun. I spontaneously moved into one yoga posture after another (I never studied yoga). I understood why earlier cultures worshiped the sun. From that moment forward, I could see auras around people (something I had never seen before). I understood why pictures in Christianity and in Buddhism often show halos around the heads of special people. Perhaps there was a time when we all saw auras. Religions of all sorts never had made sense to me before and suddenly I felt the underlying truth that is the foundation of all religions.

I had undergone a powerful and moving transformation. So this is what was meant by an enlightenment experience! Since those moments I have never been the same.

READING LIST

For more information on holotropic breathing, I recommend the book

<u>Heighten Your Holos</u> by Dr. Alex Lessin. 1991 Lessin's Lessons,
    PO Box 1223, Wailuku, Maui, Hawaii 96793

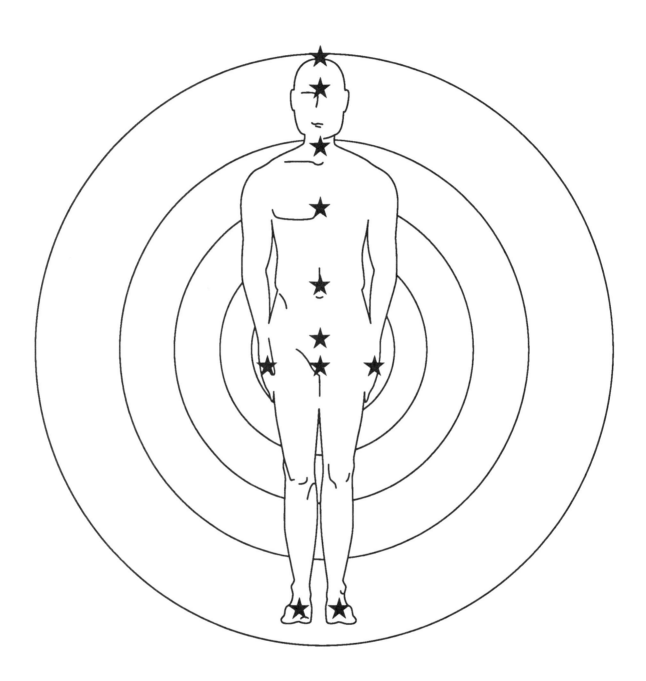

CHAPTER 6

GOOD VIBRATIONS:
VIBRATIONAL COLOR REGRESSION STYLES

A Trance-Former

Living at ohm
taking up resonance
In-chanting

There are 2 approaches to the inner journey which use your physical body energy, color and feelings to access information. They are THE SHELLEY LESSIN STOCKWELL GOOD VIBES SYSTEM and the EGYPTIAN SYSTEM OF ASSIGNED COLORS AND SYMBOLS. The third, TAKING UP RESONANCE, uses sound instead of colors to access information. All three use the physical body and chakras as stimuli for the trip.

The chakras correspond with our central nervous system and each is said to control the seven major glands of the body. The chakras follow our spinal cord from the base of the spine to the top of the head. The base of the spine, the sexual organs, and the solar plexus (gut) are often referred to as our lower chakras. Our spiritual or upper chakras are the heart, throat, third eye and the top of the head (none as 'the lotus of a thousand petals' by the ancients). The meridians charted by body workers directly relates to each chakra.

THE SHELLEY LESSIN STOCKWELL GOOD VIBES SYSTEM

I developed this system for those who feel resistance to the word hypnosis. Those who tend to be kinesthetic (touch oriented) will discover that this style taps excellent energy and is colorful as well.

HOW TO DO IT
Before you begin, look at the page with the diagram of the body's chakras.

MUSIC
Now put on some relaxing music and stretch out comfortably on your back, feet 8" to 10" apart, arms loosely and limply by your side.

BLESS ME

> Bless me on all levels
> Physically, mentally
> Emotionally and spiritually
> So I may truly
> recognize and fulfill my life's purpose.
> Let all teachings be for the highest good
> of myself and humanity.
> Help me reconnect
> with my special gifts
> and let me lovingly shed any
> negative messages given by insensitive people.
>
> Thank you.
> Amen.

TRACK YOUR BREATHING
Track your breathing by noticing each easy natural breath and allow your breath to lace gently in and out of the soothing music.

PENETRATION: ASSIGN COLORS
When you decide you would like to begin, focus your attention on the lowest chakra (your seat or base of your spine) and gradually move up the chart until you have focused on all the chakras. Assign a color to each chakra. Any color you choose. Focus your attention on the color and notice the energy in that place.

THE CHAKRAS

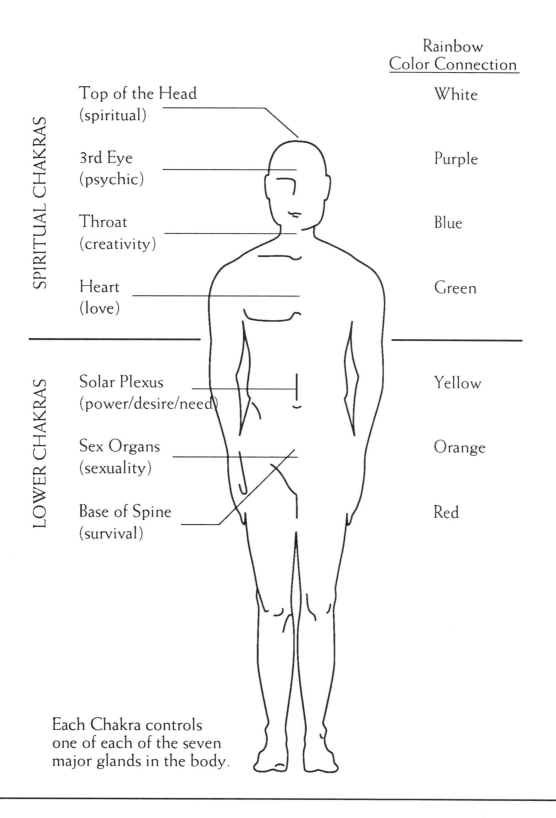

Rainbow
Color Connection

SPIRITUAL CHAKRAS

Top of the Head
(spiritual) — White

3rd Eye
(psychic) — Purple

Throat
(creativity) — Blue

Heart
(love) — Green

LOWER CHAKRAS

Solar Plexus
(power/desire/need) — Yellow

Sex Organs
(sexuality) — Orange

Base of Spine
(survival) — Red

Each Chakra controls
one of each of the seven
major glands in the body.

NOTICE VIBRATIONS

Become aware of any energy vibration or feeling at each spot. Imagine your breathing going directly to that chakra.

COMBINING ALL SENSATIONS

Combine all of these points of energy and color and notice how your entire being feels. Describe to yourself or companion how your personal vibration feels.

TRAVEL TO ANOTHER TIME

Go back to another place in time, another lifetime, where you identify this same vibration.

ASK QUESTIONS

- **Feet?** Look at your feet. This will ground you. Describe what you see Notice if you have shoes.

- **Clothes?** Notice what you are wearing or not wearing.

- **Senses?** One by one, allow your experience to enter each of your senses. Notice any smells, tastes, sounds, bodily sensations, sights and extra sensory sensations.

- **Others?** Are you alone or with someone?

- **Location?** Are you inside or outside?

- **Time?** What is the time period or year? What season is it?

- **Experience?** What is happening? What happens next?

- **Death?** Answer the question: "How did this entity die?"

- **White Light** Send that entity white light. Picture and imagine a flood of white light upon them and see what happens.

- **Learned?** "What have I learned from this lifetime" or "What message is this entity wishing to give me?"

COMING BACK

When you are ready to return to your here and now awareness, take a deep breath and stretch.

OPEN YOUR EYES

Ground yourself by using one of the methods described in "Rules of the Road".

EXAMPLES USING THE SHELLEY STOCKWELL GOOD VIBES SYSTEM

These two past life regressions manifested one following the other and were stimulated by the Shelley Stockwell Good Vibes System. I have recorded for you the colors and energies that I experienced with each chakra. Notice that I included my hands and feet. You might want to do so as well.

Base of the Spine	blue/green, deep color, heavy
Sexual organs	pink, pulsating
Solar plexus	white, lifting up, wings
Heart	green, leaves, curling
Throat	rose color, petals of a flower
3rd eye	yellow, rolling ocean
Top of the head	the sun, all the colors, pulsating light
Hands	crystal lakes
Feet	brown rocks

Sheepskin Man

Sheepskin, curly white sheepskin. Sheepskin everywhere. Flies in face, forehead. Hot. Lots of sheepskin. Wound above right eye. Sheepskin board fell and hit my head. A round stick board used to pile sheep skin. Round building stretched with skin. Sheepskin doesn't smell. Dried and hot. Waiting for Gali to bring goats milk. Very rich. The goat's eyes are strange. They pull me into their eyes. Like the blindness the flies bring, the goat's eyes are blue and clear. Gali is late. I have learned to wait. I believe that all life is simply waiting. Waiting until the next time we wait again. Stacking sheepskin and waiting. I like the mountain, the sun is hot on the mountain and I talk to the sun. My right eye does not open because of the board on my head. I was crushed to the eye. My mother lives in a white house made of stone, round. She wears skirts and has big breasts. White blouse, black braids. My mother has 2 teeth that are gray in the front and she has brown tight eyes.

John Gleason

You don't want him to know about the big tube on the ship. We made a mistake on the ship and all the people will drown. The big, round tube at the top of the ship. We don't want them to know we welded it wrong. They must never know. They will die; scream. The big chandelier will break. The captain asked me and I said I didn't know. I welded it wrong. The tube is blue and silver. 1918. 1920. My name is John Gleason. I am wearing blue pants. I have a wife with curly, brown hair and 4 little dumplings and I welded it wrong. I will never tell. I will die everyday I live. I will die with the screams, with their faces, with water coming through my nose. I will die when I am 69 but I will have died everyday.

I welded it wrong. I have a son Danny. He is a happy lad. He has a favorite dog. When I was a boy, I was like Danny. I welded it wrong. God help me. I killed all those people. I welded it wrong. I killed them I can never rest. I can never rest. I am so ashamed, so ashamed. My wife does not think I love her. It is myself I do not love. I was in charge of the workers. I wanted the work done quickly. I didn't think it would make a difference. It made a big difference. I welded it wrong. I was drinking the night before. I didn't care. The people, the children. Lusitania.

I sent him the white light. He dies. He doesn't go to God. He doesn't leave the earth. I cannot forgive him. I will send white light to his brown grave. I carry him in my feet.

Note: On May 1, 1915, the Lusitania was sunk by a German U boat. 1,255 passengers and 700 crew members died. The ship sported a large chandelier. The pleasure ship contained secret munitions known to Churchill and Roosevelt. The disaster was publically blamed on the ship's improper design and instability and the captains incompetency.

THE EGYPTIAN SYSTEM OF COLORS AND SYMBOLS

This is my variation of the "Past Life Regression" technique developed by Loy Young. Ms. Young is a world traveling Texan who believes in reincarnation. She says her original system is a combination of many techniques. She believes that her approach eliminates "the inaccuracy of imagination" by use of a simple reality check. Using an Egyptian color and chakra system you focus upon your own energy frequency or vibration and take it back to another place in time.

HOW TO DO IT

MEMORY CHECK
Establish the difference between imagination and memory:

1. Imagine something that really didn't happen.
2. Imagine something that did.

Now that you know the difference between imagination and memory, you choose to journey into your memory and not your imagination.

BLESS ME

> Bless me on all levels
> Physically, mentally

Emotionally and spiritually
So I may truly
recognize and fulfill my life's purpose.
Let all teachings be for the highest good
of myself and humanity.
Help me reconnect
with my special gifts
and let me lovingly shed any
negative messages given by insensitive people.

Thank you.
Amen.

INDUCTION

Tense and relax each part of your body starting with your feet and moving up to your face. Now tense your entire body hold it, count slowly to 5 and take a deep breath...and let it go.

PENETRATION

Now, penetrate each color and pull it to you. After each color, describe your feelings. Describe the colors.

Start with the **base of your spine** thinking of the color **green** and let green match with the feeling of **healing**. Describe the color green. Express a word to best describe that feeling.

Now focus on the **pubic bone** and bring in the color **red** to stand for the feeling of **courage**. Describe the color red. Match the vibration to the color and express a word to best describe that energy.

Now to the **solar plexus** (above navel) and the color **blue**. Blue serves as an anchor for past lives and goes with the word **feelings**. Now a word for that energy and describe the color.

Next the **heart** and the color **lilac** to go with the feeling of **love** and **emotional** healing and then a word to describe your feelings on that body plane.

Now the **throat** and **yellow** to move you through the effects of **illusion** and your word for this feeling.

The **forehead** or 3rd eye and saffron **orange** are next and go with the feeling of **pioneering**. Now a word for this feeling and describe the color.
Now the **top of the head** and royal **purple** to bring you to the **spiritual** plane and a word to describe your energy there and that color.

```
EGYPTIAN CHAKRA, COLOR AND SYMBOL ASSIGNMENT

        CHAKRA          COLOR          ENERGY

        Seat            Green          Healing
        Pubic           Red            Courage
        Solar Plexus    Blue           Feelings
        Heart           Lilac          Love
        Throat          Yellow         Illusion
        3rd Eye         Orange         Pioneering
        Top of Head     White          Spirituality
```

COMBINING ALL THESE SENSATIONS

Combine all of these points of energy and color and notice how your entire being feels. Describe to yourself or companion how your personal vibration feels.

TRAVEL TO ANOTHER TIME

Take a deep breath. Go back to another place in time, another lifetime, where you identify this same vibration.

COMING BACK

When you are ready to return to your here and now awareness, take a deep breath and stretch.

OPEN YOUR EYES

Ground yourself by using one of the methods described in "Rules of the Road".

EXAMPLES USING THE EGYPTIAN SYSTEM OF COLORS AND SYMBOLS

Here is what happened when I used the Egyptian system of colors and symbols.

Green	green plant, bud. Yellowish green feeling - crunch.
Red	bright, raisin like the sun - excitement
Blue	turquoise splashed across the sky - deep peace
Lilac	very soft lilac - serenity
Yellow	mustard yellow - yuk
Orange	sunset - hope
Purple	too bright to see - expansive
Combination of all colors & energies	illuminous, radiant, energized

Greek Man

I'm seeing a cross. Not a Christian cross. A square cross. A religion. No name. Nameless. It's secret. It's dangerous, no one can know. It's either not real (I made it up) or the enemy will say it's not the right religion.

I'm not really crazy - I don't think - a lot of people think I'm crazy. It's my religion - it's against Christ. I made my cross different. They put me in a place with all these people who are crazy. It's on an island. I'm not really crazy, when I was a little boy in the village I was the smartest little boy and I didn't believe in the cross. Priest told us Christ was God not earth and sky. So I made our cross and put it outside so they could see they were crazy to say I was crazy. Otherwise they would kill me and my family.

I'm here with all these people. Some are nice. I still worship my cross - some worship with me. Some can't talk or think. I think I'll die here in this place. Nice weather here. I like the ocean and the food. And I like the lady with the white hair. We sleep together at night. I don't know if she's crazy or not. She feels nice. I'm 61. It's pretty boring here. Like my turtle life - slow and boring. I'm comfortable and I don't have to do anything. I go to the sea, I like the turtles there. They remind me of me. That's all.

(What did you learn in this lifetime?)

Stand by what you believe as truth. even the punishment has it's rewards. That is peace. Stand by what you believe.

Cowboy

Seeing lots of colors, lots of shapes. Red dripping down. Orange dripping down. Red. Its a heart. I can see the heart beating. I want to touch it. I'm afraid to touch it. Now I'm inside the heart. I am totally disoriented. I don't know what's going on.

Now I see a horse outside. Sweaty. Drips of sweat are running down it's neck. The horse is brown with white splotches. It just ran really fast. Dak, I call him Dak. I was riding him. My chaps are sweaty. My balls are sore. My legs hurt. It takes a while to walk straight after riding. People laugh about cowboys being bowlegged. It's true. Your legs hurt after you get off the horse. They are like that for about an hour. People say cowboys like the smell of cowshit. I don't like it. The flies are annoying. I don't like the smell of Dak or me. It can be bitter cold here. And the smells are never good. I live near the slaughterhouse. I slaughter cows and bulls. The worse part is to see the hearts beating. The hearts beat after they are slaughtered. Something is wrong when you see the life force still pumping. But man's got to eat. Nothing is as fine as a big, thick, juicy steak.

The old porch is crumbling. It used to be white. Now, it's just a pile of splinters glued together. Termite wood. Nothing keeps up here. Not the cows. Not the homestead. Not man, woman, or child. Wyoming here. There are sores on my head from sweating in my hat. I think its from hard soap. You never can wash it out just right. My hair is going gray now. It is getting thin on the sides. I used to have a big head of hair. I used to be proud of my hair.

Dave Daniels grabbed me by my hair once in town. I kicked him good with the point of my boot. He sneers at me now. He never grabbed me again.

I'm pretty lonely. Don't think much about it. My life is just mud on boots, fields of cow patties and those damn flies.

My Ma and Pa came across in a covered wagon. I wasn't even a twinkle in my Pa's eye he used to say. Why they chose to settle in this God forsaken place, I don't have any idea. The biggest thing that ever happens is when the carnival comes. It comes every three years. All those slickers and round hats. Yelling and hawking. It don't do much for loneliness. See all them pretty gals. I like Becky. This ain't no life for Becky. Cow guts. Cow shit. Hay. Maybe I'll get my own wagon and be like Ma and Pa and head across country. Find us a greener pasture.

(How did he die?) He died in a big red leather chair in Philadelphia in his sister Sara's house at the age of 58. He died with his boots on. His boots were clean.

(Send him the light) I send him the light. His energy leaves through his shoulders. It goes to God.

(What did I learn?) I learned to love animals. His heart felt their hearts.

TAKING UP RESONANCE: THE SOUND APPROACH

Do this approach in a place where you have privacy so the sounds you make won't disturb others.

HOW TO DO IT

NO MUSIC (you will make your own)

BLESS ME

> Bless me on all levels
> Physically, mentally
> Emotionally and spiritually
> So I may truly
> recognize and fulfill my life's purpose.
> Let all teachings be for the highest good
> of myself and humanity.
> Help me reconnect
> with my special gifts
> and let me lovingly shed any
> negative messages given by insensitive people.
>
> Thank you.
> Amen.

SING YOUR NAME

Sing your name out loud. Say your name in any rhythm and feel the vibration of the sound. Repeat the sound of your name and vibration 5 times.

LET OUT SOUNDS

1. Take a deep breath. Let it out. Let out any sound and vibration, starting from the bottoms of your feet. Repeat the sound.

2. Move up to the knees. Let the sound, the breath and the energy move fully and openly. Repeat the sound.

3. Move up to your hips. Again, let the sound and energy move openly. Repeat the sound.

4. Now, move to your stomach. Repeat.

5. Next is your chest. Repeat.

6. Shoulders.

7. Arms

8. Hands

9. Throat

10. Jaw

11. Nasal Cavaties

12. Forehead

13. Ears

14. Skull

Combine all of these chakras together. Let out the sound and notice the vibrations. Repeat the sound 4 times.

TRAVEL TO ANOTHER TIME

Go back, back, back in times to a similar sound, a similavibration. Invite any sensations to emerge.

ASK YOUR QUESTIONS

• Feet?	Look at your feet. This will ground you. Describe what you see Notice if you have shoes.
• Clothes?	Notice what you are wearing or not wearing.
• Senses?	One by one, allow your experience to enter each of your senses. Notice any smells, tastes, sounds, bodily sensations,sights and extra sensory sensations.
• Others?	Are you alone or with someone?
• Location?	Are you inside or outside?
• Time?	What is the time period or year? What season is it?
• Experience?	What is happening? What happens next?
• Death?	Answer the question: "How did this entity die?"
• White Light	Send that entity white light. Picture and imagine a flood of white light upon them and see what happens.
• Learned?	"What have I learned from this lifetime" or "What message is this entity wishing to give me?

COME ON BACK

OPEN YOUR EYES AND GROUND YOURSELF

EXAMPLE USING THE SOUND APPROACH

Brown Bear (1990)

I'm in a cave. Light is at the end of the cave. It smells of earth and brown bears. I'm a brown bear. Big, brown bear. I have big feet. I'm heavy. I like to fall over on my heavy body. My big feet are tired of carrying me around. Big, big, big brown bear.

I like being a bear. There's a moth. I like to bat at moths and play with them. I stay away from bats. They hurt you. The red/green berries are good. The Indians eat them too. I climbed up a tree and saw lots of berries in a papoose case. I got them - ripped it open with my claws. The skin ripped. I ate so many berries. I went back in the cave. I could sleep. I like to sleep and eat berries and play. My claws and teeth are yellow and strong. I like to scare things with my big teeth. They yell and run away.

Big, heavy, ambling bear. Clomp. Clomp. Clomp. That's the sound my feet make. Grasses tickle my feet in the mud. Mud is nice and cool on hot days. I roll in the mud on hot days. It feels good.

Brown bear. Big, old, brown bear. Thick, brown. Don't like when the stickers get in. I watch people. But I stay away from the Indians and I sometimes steal their food. It's no problem.

Brown Bear (1986)
(The same bear accessed using the Touch Approach four years earlier.)

I am power. I am a bear. I'm a very brown bear. I like to lie on my back, my back itches. Brown, brown, brown bear. I like to swat at things with my claws. I like to go in the mud. Real nice - big. I waddle when I walk - I growl and I bite. I have a nice time. I like to bite at nothing, biting in air and growl. There's cold rocks I like to lie on. I got other bears sometimes. When I get mad I growl and everybody runs. I think it's funny. I'm a nice bear. Everyone is scared. I like to eat meat. I eat meat - sticks to my teeth. I bite other animals. I kill them. I jump on them and put my teeth in their back. Sometimes they kick and make noise. I eat them up with their bones. I eat chunks of meat not bones. Animals with white on the tail that wiggles. My front paw hurts halfway up. Hurts. I got kicked there. It hurts. Funny animal with white tail kicked me.

Pregnant Bird

Drifting over the ocean I see a heart made of light and the water and the land. I hear the ocean. I'm pregnant. Don't think birds get pregnant. I'm over the water. Pregnant, nice and juicy with baby in my tummy and I feel real - it's crazy. I think I have a bear in my stomach. Brown bear. Juicy, baby brown bear. Think I'm a bird but I act like a brown bear. Feel like a bear but I'm a bird. Fun flying over wall.

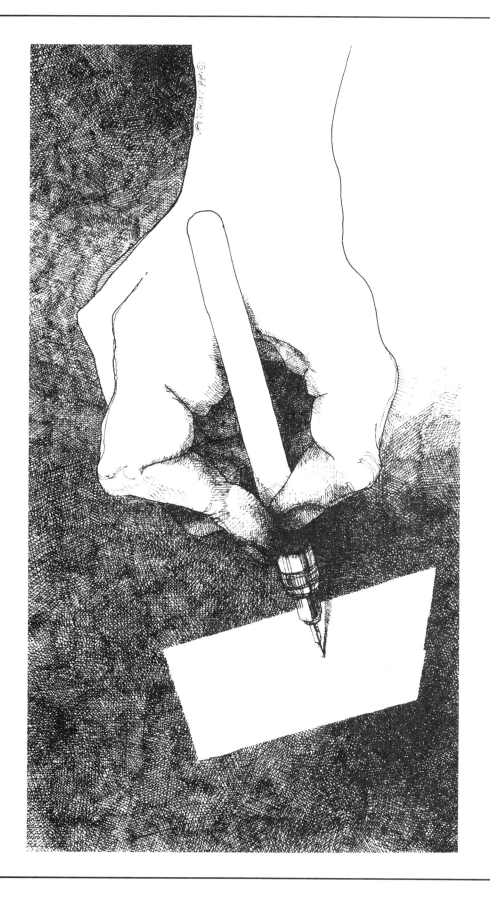

CHAPTER 7

THE MAGIC TOUCH
AUTOMATIC WRITING • MASSAGE

Who in the world is in here now?
For heavens sake and holy cow.
Why is it a sub personality
dressed as God inside of me!

Tactile folks experience touch as a powerful stimulus for deep mind response. In this chapter, we will demystify AUTOMATIC WRITING and two whole body touch approaches: SELF MASSAGE and THE FRIENDLY MASSAGE.

AUTOMATIC WRITING

Words can make a tremendous difference in how we say things.

Automatic writing has been used as a style of inner communication with the subconscious mind and one's creative essence, since the beginning of recorded history. The ancient Chinese used a planchette (which is a Ouija board like contraption with a writing implement attached). Emerson and Beethoven both claimed that their creative essence moved through their body onto paper from a "unseen source". The <u>Rhyme of the</u>

Ancient Mariner by Herman Melville was written by automatic writing as was the Urantha Book. The Impersonal Life, written in 1916, was proported to be "channeled" (written) through the author from an outside source. In 1930, psychiatrist Virginia Moll wrote detailed reports on the power of automatic writing as a therapeutic tool and said anyone can learn how to do it and benefit.

This style of inner journey takes various forms, from journal writing at one end to having written something and been totally unaware of that process of writing (as if from a deep trance state).

HOW TO DO IT

As with all the processes in this book, there are no right or wrong ways to do automatic writing. Whatever your style, it will be perfect. Choose the media that you want to use. You may use paper and pencil or a typewriter. If you don't know how to type before you begin this process, you probably won't know how during the process.

Everyone's technique is different. You may discover that you write with your dominant or non-dominant hand. Some people actually write with both hands "mirror style", each hand writing an entirely different message at the same time!

Your handwriting will probably be larger and more cursive than your normal pattern. The words will probably run together. Your writing will be rapid, larger, and scrawlier. Often the "i's" aren't dotted and the "t's" aren't crossed and punctuation is forgotten. Some people actually write vertically and move in patterns around the paper never having to pick up their pencil. Doodlers and dreamers make excellent automatic writers.

PAPER
Abundance is the word to describe your paper. Make sure you have lots of it.

GET COMFORTABLE
Sit comfortably in a place where you will not be disturbed.

BLESS ME

> Bless me on all levels
> Physically, mentally
> Emotionally and spiritually
> So I may truly
> recognize and fulfill my life's purpose.
> Let all teachings be for the highest good
> of myself and humanity.
> Help me reconnect

with my special gifts
and let me lovingly shed any
negative messages given by insensitive people.

Thank you.
Amen.

BEGIN THE JOURNEY

Close your eyes and imagine going to a beautiful place in nature. Somewhere that brings you a feeling of peace and serenity. Experience this place from any one or all of your senses. Enjoy the smells, colors, tastes, breezes, and sights. Now imagine going into a special room (you are the designer) and waiting for you inside is your own personal inner guide. The guide could be any form that you imagine. Have them hand you a computer disk. Take that disk to another room and give it to the automatic writing librarian who places it in your deepest mind.

ASK FOR INFORMATION

You may automatic write with no structured plan or you may ask a question of yourself. The information will emerge from your deepest wisdom. Ask for information back in time and past life images will emerge to help you understand and fulfill your purpose in living. You may even ask to "talk" with a loved one who has died.

BEGIN WRITING

Now, take a deep, full breath and let it out. Don't judge or analyze or think. When you begin writing, simply let all impulses go through your nervous system through the pen and to the paper. Let your pen move on the paper as if it had a life of it's own. Let it be. At first, it might be scribbles or lines, or random words. Let them come. No matter what, don't stop. Just let it come. Eventually you will find messages - lots of them.

PRACTICE MAKES PERFECT

As with anything in life you get better with practice each time you do this process. You will find that more and more will flow and each session will take on a different flavor than any other one.

EXAMPLES USING AUTOMATIC WRITING

Here is two past lives that I accessed using automatic writing:

Gary Oldsten

Gary Oldsten of the great greenest of Greenland. Open to sea, sand, standing alone by the sea, my sea made for me. Seaweed, shells, I like to walk upon the sand. Cold grains in my toes, I will die barefoot of cold before I am old. I am always slightly alone. My right foot gimp, drags sand trails to the sea. Pop the seaweed poppers, that's my music calamity.

My mothers, she has yellow hair like pale lemons in the sun, long days in the sun. White walls in an island in Greek lands. Small and tidy, my island. Abraxus is it's name. I eat pomegranates and paint my gimp foot red. Octopus and squid are rare delights. My mouth drips with ooze and squid. My father likes to dance in the hall with red-lipped lady of the night. His hair is white and smells of pipe. My dog is gray and stupid and fine. I have a lip tucked tight above and speak tight and my teeth hurt, lowers crushed upon uppers to my nose. I am alone on my sandy beach looking at a million stars. I die on this beach from drinking salt and learn that I have melted sand. I reach a silent beach.

Bison

How do you do this and that. How do you go into and out of awareness and don't care. I am holy holy holy. Jaw tight, throat tight, going in and out of buffalo. Buffalo horns upon my head, my crown for (king to some) buffalo prince in our land of smoke mountains and sage caves. My head hurts. Like the bison I wear I have to suffer for my food. The bison gave his life. I wear his horns and head upon my own. His life is within me. Food from the great white clouds, food of life runs through the river, the sun. The bison up from now to forever. The bison and man locked like interlaced branches of trees. Like finger on hands. Bison God. Bison Food. Bison Life.

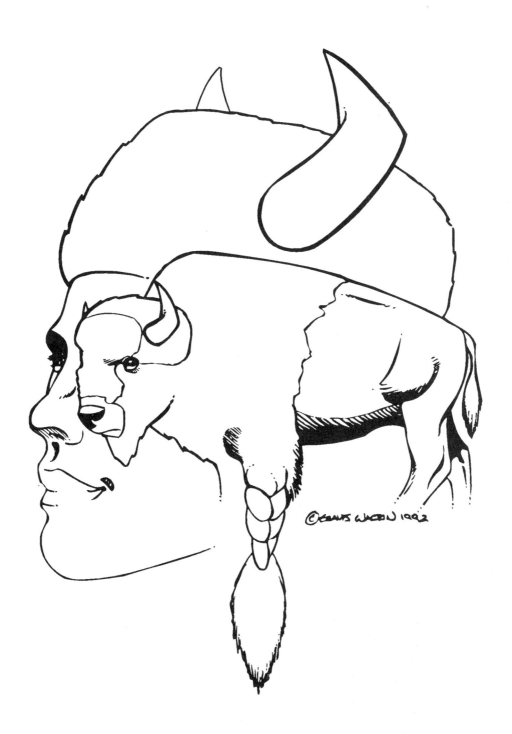

Since poetry is my preferred style of communication, I automatic wrote this:

The Girl In The Middle

I am going to die. Oh, why must I die?
I love living clinging upon me
like spider webs tickling my nose
I want to feel the grass in my toes.

The pollen is strong;
(yellow crumbs of life sprinkled on little bee legs)
I want to be.
I want to stay sprinkled on earth.
I don't want to go or leave you; (you of my heart)
You are my heart.
I have struggled to love this body (where I dwell)
This body which has transported
my heart and soul and thoughts.
I don't want you to leave me body
after we finally got to love again.

If I go (torn from you)
what will become of our dreams?
Our visions of tomorrows?
Our time to laugh
and our deep sorrows?

I have no control and I want to control.
I want to choose that I have no choice.
I have no choice.

I want to go back
back to the years of tender corn
(waving in fields, steamy and warm)
back to the earth
(hot, mud parched, dry)
back to the mama and apple pie.
Back to the checkered table cloth
and coffee (black as sin)
back to the swing (the big white swing)
creaky in the hot summer night.
Sweat smells sweet like tea.
And the children in white frocks
skip-the-loop upon the brown grass.

Jonas, Becky come to the fair.

The barker came. The clown is there.
Joelly and Barbara and Cary Ann,
will take you back where everyone can
dance and swing and play the fiddle
and I can love the girl in the middle.

Why do I write this gibber posh pie?
Why am I in this stew?
Tell me what is wrong with me.
What am I to do?

So give me a plumcake and apple flap
and I will give you my love back.

Jessica

This is a fascinating example of "channeled" automatic writing. Jessica Kaitlin Morris left the earth plane at the tender age of four. Her mother, Diane, spontaneously began automatic "channeling" Jessica shortly after she departed.

Over the course of 6 months, "Jessica's" writing got more structured and mature. Here is a thank you letter that I received recently from Diane. Notice the shift in writing style as Jessica's automatic writing came through.

THE TOUCH APPROACH

Centuries ago, Mongolian warriors used self massage before battle. You can massage any part of the body you can reach using any stroke you choose.

Shiatsu massage involves pressure on the acupuncture points in order to balance the body's energy and create good health. Shiatsu simply means "finger pressure". It's origins date back some 4,000 years in the Orient. They call the kundalini energy or vital source: "ki". Ki energy is seen as a system of "meridians" each connected to a part of the body. Meridians are actually the channels through which the "ki" flow through the body.

Many masseurs, acupuncturists, and chiropractors find that their clients access vivid regressions.

SELF MASSAGE

HOW TO DO IT:

Close your eyes as you massage the following in sequential order. Remember to breathe fully into the spot you are massaging and say to yourself "going back in time".

MUSIC

Put on nice music.

BLESS ME

> Bless me on all levels
> Physically, mentally
> Emotionally and spiritually
> So I may truly
> recognize and fulfill my life's purpose.
> Let all teachings be for the highest good
> of myself and humanity.
> Help me reconnect
> with my special gifts
> and let me lovingly shed any
> negative messages given by insensitive people.
>
> Thank you.
> Amen.

TOES, FEET, LEGS

Starting with your left foot first, milk each toe, pulling it with your thumb and forefinger firmly from the root of the toe to the tip of your toe. Work from the big toe out to the smallest, one at a time. You may use lotion or massage oil, but I prefer not to use anything.

Move on to the top and bottom of your foot. Apply as much pressure as you would like. Follow the contours of your Achilles heel and bring the energy and your strokes up the leg to your knee. Move up your thigh, particularly focusing on your hips on that side. You might like to turn over on one side while working the hip.

Now, move to the right foot. Repeat the process.

ABDOMEN

Lay flat on your back. Use a pillow if you like. Now gently massage your abdomen. Massage in a large circular motion, using both hands. Work under the rib cage, gently kneading and pressing. Notice that your hands may become warmer. Encourage that energy to move from your hands into the abdomen. Take a long time here.

HEART

Move now to the heart. Lay your hands upon your breast bone. Become aware of the sensation of your heart beating.

HANDS AND ARMS

Work on your hands and arms if you like.

NECK AND SHOULDERS

Work your way up towards the neck and shoulders, gently massaging and noticing the warmth of your hands.Spend extra time on your neck, particularly where your neck connects to your skull. With a circular motion massage your scalp, moving from around the ears, all the way up to the top of your head.

FACE

With your two forefingers, move across the bridge of your nose, up into the brow bone above your eyes and gently press. Remember to keep breathing. Linger there.

Cup your hands over your eyes with the palms of your hands, forming a cavity above your closed eyes. Count back from 10 to 1 slowly. Take a full breath with each count and then place a finger firmly on the space between your two eyebrows (third eye). Press firmly and say your blessing.

Note: If there is any place that has pain or discomfort, stay there and let any information come from that place.The discomfort will release.

GO BACK TO ANOTHER TIME

ASK QUESTIONS

- **Feet?** — Look at your feet. This will ground you. Describe what you see Notice if you have shoes.

- **Clothes?** — Notice what you are wearing or not wearing.

- **Senses?** — One by one, allow your experience to enter each of your senses. Notice any smells, tastes, sounds, bodily sensations, sights and extra sensory sensations.

- **Others?** — Are you alone or with someone?

- **Location?** — Are you inside or outside?

- **Time?** — What is the time period or year? What season is it?

- **Experience?** — What is happening? What happens next?

- **Death?** — Answer the question: "How did this entity die?"

- **White Light** — Send that entity white light. Picture and imagine a flood of white light upon them and see what happens.

- **Learned?** — "What have I learned from this lifetime" or "What message is this entity wishing to give me?"

OPEN YOUR EYES AND COME ON BACK

When you are ready to return to your here and now awareness. Take a deep breath and stretch. Remember to ground yourself.

EXAMPLES USING SELF-MASSAGE

Opium Girl

I see a dog jumping across the sand. Playing on the sand. Going down very deep. Eats sweet melons. Very sweet melons. Keep the flies away. We feed the master sweet melons and dates. Sara, little Sara. Don't know if she's real or not. Don't understand all the languages. Silver plates. You wear shoes with turned up toes and bells. Some gold, some silver bells. Purple brocade. Sara is a child. She brings the master teacakes on a tray. Maybe she is not real. Maybe she is just a toy mouse. Nothing is real. Everything feels like a dream. We are always smoking opium from the big pipes. We always lay back on the big pillows.

For as long as we can remember, which isn't very long, our time is opium and smoke. Our time flows up in smoke. Opium goes through our blood. Opium is our lover. Clouds of thoughts. Clouds of smoke. Blue and purple brocade. Shoes with bells on the toes. They say there is fighting but we don't care. We are with opium in the large room with master. It is quiet here. Little Sara is real. It is we who are not. She comes and brings food. That is me when I was small. How did I get to be here in clouds of smoke. Little Sara. Drift off. She had pure shiny eyes and rings of curls that bounced on her pretty head. She wore pink brocade, bloom pants, fitted at the ankle. Pretty little shoes with bells. The crown hat, like a beehive and a star at the point. Her mother would pinch her. Her mother was nasty and would tell her to serve the master and be quick about it. Father would sneer with black teeth that were broken. Sara wore a little white smock apron and served the teacakes. Saltanis. Once it painted her fingernails purple with grapes. She liked that. She didn't like to go to bed at night on the straw. She was cold. The smoke hurts her eyes. How did I become like this. Opium to the floor. Opium mist floated on mist. Master rarely talks. He is opium to the floor. When he falls off the platform it is very difficult to move him but we move like a segmented worm. We move and push him back upon the pillow platform. The pillows are pink and purple brocade. The ceiling is tent. Bedawon tent. My name is Darcy but it was Sara. The life is smoked out of me like the others. Too big to move, nothing will ever change. I have a headache above my right eye from the opium. My mouth is dry. I would ring for tea if I could. Maybe Sara will come again. She was a good little girl. Her mother pinched her cheeks too hard. Her father was a dirty man.

She died in the pillows. No one knew how old she was but she was older than her years.

I send her the light but she can't have it. She can't go. She must learn first. They throw her body in a pit upon other bones and they throw a dead camel on top. She is still there. It is in Pakistan. Pali Pakistan.

I am having difficulty finding out what she wants me to learn. Her message is to come back to Sara and to stay away from fire and smoke. Stay away from opium. It is a life of death. Worse than death. It is no life at all.

Desert Boy

Trouble with eyes. My eyes have sand in them, my butt as sand in it. There's a lot of sand. My eyes are having trouble. Can't get the sand out. I think I'm blind - I'm hot - I'm thirsty and I can't see. The sand is not bothering me anymore. I think the sand made me blind. It was horrible sand. It burned my skin and made me blind.

(Why did you choose to be in the sand?)

I had to go with my father. I had to go with my father. To lead the camel for my father. I am very hot and I cannot lead the camel anymore.

I'm left, I feel alone. I'm very thirsty. Very, very thirsty. I'm gong to die of thirst. So hot, very weak and I can't see. I think I will die here. I can't be this thirsty anymore - so hot. My brain is drying up, I can see the angels.

(Look down at the dead person)

It's a little boy, Looks like a sheet on him and rope, He's a little boy with very brown skin - the color of camel fur - black hair. He's a handsome little boy - his eyes don't work anymore. He looks like a puddle in a sheet. He was a nice little boy.

THE FRIENDLY MASSAGE

This approach is done with help from a friend or body worker. Trager, Shiatsu, Rolfing, Energy Balancing and Reflexology Massages with someone of like mind enhance your time travel journey.

HOW TO DO IT:

MUSIC
Put on some nice music.

BLESS ME

> Bless me on all levels
> Physically, mentally
> Emotionally and spiritually
> So I may truly
> recognize and fulfill my life's purpose.
> Let all teachings be for the highest good
> of myself and humanity.
> Help me reconnect
> with my special gifts
> and let me lovingly shed any
> negative messages given by insensitive people.
>
> Thank you.
> Amen.

BEGIN YOUR MASSAGE

Take a deep breath, lie on your stomach and have your friend touch your body in the following sequential order. Take your time and as you touch each part of the body, notice any colors, images, or feelings that surface.

TALK TO YOUR BUDDY

Communicate how hard or soft to massage or if you need more time in one spot. Let out any sound or words that correspond to that spot. Tape record the session or decode it to remember it clearly or write it down afterwards.

EXAMPLES USING THE FRIENDLY MASSAGE

Monkey/Man
(1986 Shiatsu - Energy Balancing)
(Shiatsu uses touch and a system of pressure points similar to acupuncture)

I don't like flies. I'm very uncomfortable. I think I've been tied down. Somewhere between here and there. I keep seeing a green flat thing (looks like a flat balloon made of metal) used to tie me up there.

My body feels stiff - stiff - itchy and stiff. I have to move around now. I can't stay like this, I have to move around now. I can't stay like this. I have to move around. I have to do this because of religion. I'm very uncomfortable. I've got to move. I got to move. I got to get out of here - not comfortable. I'm very uncomfortable. I'm hot, got to stay in same position. Sometimes I've been told stay in same position because of religion. It itches. Not comfortable. Hot around my neck. Very uncomfortable. My feet are very big. Not an ape; not a man; in the middle.

I don't know where I am, not a man, not an ape...must be nothing. I am nothing. Staying in this form. I'm very uncomfortable. Same position for a long time. Must be brambles that itch. Very uncomfortable. Brambles scratch me. Itch. I want to hibernate. in a cave. I have brambles. Very uncomfortable here. They said the great spirit made the rule. I have to be here for a long time before I am let out and become part of the elders. My passage to elder, to whatever we are. Not man, not ape. Something. Nothing. Lots of us. Brambles in here and green thing.

Back in the sunshine the others are smiling. They let me out. The others, they have snouts like me and eyes like apes and lots of brown hair. Some have woolly, some have waves. The one with the old hair and broken tooth. The old one; he is very happy. I am out! I am happy too. I am now one of the elders.

Sun feels very good It will heal me from the brambles. They are hugging me. I don't want to go in there again. A big celebration now. My mother is there making food. Mother has little brown eyes like the lemur. Feelings for me. She is very proud I did it. My father, he's in a tree. He looks at me, he is proud too. I am an elder, too, like my father. Did it. Don't know what I am.

They are nothing. I like the little ones. They run in circles and yell. I am tired. I will sleep in the sun. I did it.

Indian
(1990 Swedish Massage)

Spine: tree trunk - birch tree
Base of spine - wings
shoulders:

Someone is being impaled on a stake. A birch stake. It is an Indian rite of manhood to let the stake go through the shoulder. To heal it, they take mushroom powder and gypsum root. When the mold forms to black mold, we take it on the sacred logs and we stick the stake through our shoulder. I'm very brave. I am brave. White Oak. 16. 16. My father must not know that I hurt. I am brave. We take pitch from trees and put them on the wounds. The scars are round and full. I am proud. We live in birch bark huts along the stream. There are many deer. My mother wears two braids and grounds the corn. She does not like to talk or smile. She has a deep sorrow. Something terrible has happened in her life.

Girl
(1990 Swedish Massage)

The town is burning. The streets are in flames. People are running. It is a terrible fire. Even the cobblestones are hot. The roofs are made of straw thatch. They burn quickly. People are running. We've come to the central square. We are in the fountain. We ran like rats. King Edward is here in his carriage to look at the smoldering buildings. He has a brown porkchop beard and fat cheeks. I laugh because I see real pork chops on his face. His hat is velvet with fur, white and brown fur, in little pieces. I'm holding my brother David's hand and my mother is behind us. Her name is Cara. I'm 5. My mother says not to be afraid. The King will protect us. I think he smiled at me. We were going to eat mutton for dinner before the big fire. It is very cold.

She died of a disease when she was 32. The rats brought it. Many died. She was a plump lady. She wore a toadstool hat, white. She baked bread. The Yolder house. She got sick and weak. Fell in the street.

I send her the light and she leaves laughing to the sun. Very funny. She always thought everything was funny.

She liked the big fire. It was exciting. She taught me to stay curious and see the humor in everything. When she saw the king with the porkchop beard, she imagined they were real porkchops glued on his face. Very funny.

Grenshla
(1990 Trager with Kathleen Zuhde)

(Tragering is a gentle lifting and "rocking" psycho physical opening process)

Black lady with rings on her neck - all different colors. Grenshla. Black hair - curly. Large lips. She flicks her lips together in language (clicks as if speaking an unusual language). She is in a forest with monkeys. She is the monkey lady. She doesn't do well with rings on her neck. They cause her pain. The others don't like her. She doesn't have a village. She is very lonely. Her parents didn't want her. They wanted to eat her monkey and she ran away with it. She lives a singular life. She is a little crazy. Stretched her neck and hurt her brain.

She dies when she is 27 years old. A monkey lifts up her arm and it falls down.

I send her the light. She dances. Her brain was hurt.

(Her message is that Shelley's brain isn't hurt.)

Jean Jarrett
(1990 Swedish Massage)

I see red robins. I draw pictures. I am an artist. I draw red robins. I like to paint red robins. I like the poem about Robin Redbreast. My father taught me to paint. You ever see birds fly when they are in a big group. My dad had pigeons. They would all fly in a circle. Very fun. I really like robins.

I made a tapestry with robins. Hundreds of robins. It hangs in the big hall. They say my birds are the most beautiful birds. I name my little girl Robin Renee. People like roses better than robins. So I paint roses. But robins are what I like the best. They fly, red stripes across the sky. They dance when they walk. Robins are smiles that live in the sky. When I die, I want to fly just like the robins. Sometimes I believe I can fly. My last name is Jarrett. Garland is my father. Rose is my mother. I can't remember my name.

She was a fabulous artist. A little obsessed with robins. She stayed up late at night to draw robins. Stitch robins. Paint robins. She even wrote poems about robins.

She died when she was 54. She drowned in a big vat. She was pushed in and died. Someone was stealing things. She died happy. She thought that God would send a robin to carry her up to heaven. She evaporated in the white light. She taught me the beauty of birds and how to be an artist. Her name was Jean.

READING LIST

<u>The Book of Massage</u> by Lucinda Lidell; Simon and Schuster, New York.
   Very good examples for massaging pressure points of foot and face.
   Great pictures.

<u>Joy's Way</u> by Brough Joy

CHAPTER 8

INNER VISIONS

A hand of vapor
A brush of mist
A mind of music
A breath of kiss.

My guide is you
My guide is me
My guide is the road
that moves me free.

His body is male
and woman with child
His energy calm
His passion wild.

A voice of dreams
A tongue of dew
A laugh of thunder
The color is blue.

Closing your eyes to the outside world helps you focus within to the amazing three dimensional hologram movies of the subconscious. Make a movie date with yourself and enjoy self love and popcorn when you are through. <u>Non-directed and Self-directed Movies</u> are easy and fun. Roll em!

NON DIRECTED MOVIES

HOW TO DO IT
Before you begin, decide the journey you want to take and what you would like to learn.

MUSIC
Play soft music and turn on the tape recorder to capture your journey.

BLESS ME

> Bless me on all levels
> Physically, mentally
> Emotionally and spiritually
> So I may truly
> recognize and fulfill my life's purpose.
> Let all teachings be for the highest good
> of myself and humanity.
> Help me reconnect
> with my special gifts
> and let me lovingly shed any
> negative messages given by insensitive people.
>
> Thank you.
> Amen.

GET COMFORTABLE
Close your eyes. Touch your thumb and forefinger together on one hand. Get comfortable. Let your breathing be easy and relaxed.

PICTURE A SETTING
Picture in your mind a perfect, beautiful setting. A beautiful place you may have seen before or one from your imagination.

DESCRIBE SETTING

Picture the setting in its entirety. First picture all the colors and shapes and report what you see out loud if using a tape recorder or having someone scribe for you. Notice what is on the ground. Notice what is on the horizon. Notice what is in the sky.

PICTURE THE THEATER

Imagine walking into this beautiful scene so that you may attend a movie. Since this is your own private movie, you need your own private theater, especially built just for you. Go ahead. Put up the walls anyway you choose. Put up the ceilings, the doors and the windows. The location of the building is exactly where you want it to be in that scene.

WATCH THE MOVIE

It is time to go inside and watch the movie titled "My Journey in Time". Walking into the theater, you are the only one inside. This is a private showing, just for you.

BEGIN YOUR JOURNEY

Get comfortable. Now look up at the big screen. When you are ready, take a nice deep breath and begin watching the movies behind your eyes. Keep saying to yourself "Go back, go back in time."

ASK QUESTIONS

- Feet?   Look at your feet. This will ground you. Describe what you see Notice if you have shoes.

- Clothes?   Notice what you are wearing or not wearing.

- Senses?   One by one, allow your experience to enter each of your senses. Notice any smells, tastes, sounds, bodily sensations,sights and extra sensory sensations.

- Others?   Are you alone or with someone?

- Location?   Are you inside or outside?

- Time?   What is the time period or year? What season is it?

- Experience?   What is happening? What happens next?

- Death?   Answer the question: "How did this entity die?"

- White Light   Send that entity white light. Picture and imagine a flood of white light upon them and see what happens.

- Learned?   "What have I learned from this lifetime" or "What message is this entity wishing to give me?"

OPEN YOUR EYES AND COME ON BACK

GROUND YOURSELF
Get grounded by taking a vinegar bath. Give yourself some time to be with yourself.

EXAMPLE USING NON-DIRECTED MOVIE APPROACH

Leonard Broderick

Stowaway. Disgusting. The ship smells. God awful ship. Lubela, the Pride of Belgium. Red bandanna around his neck. He is sick, barfing. He is sitting on wheat bags and is throwing up on them. Even the rats are leaving him alone. He is 16 years old. His name is Leonard Broderick. He doesn't know how to read. He got knifed on the left side of his gut before he got on the ship. He was thrown on the ship. Now they ignore him.

"I'm going to America. For a long time I've wanted to go." He plays the accordion, painted red on each side. He looks like on of the people in Van Gogh's "The Potato Eaters".

He's poor - nauseated again. He drinks too much beer. There is a big scar where he was knifed. Uses coppers to buy beer (Shelley laughs). He's funny, a showman. He's dancing and playing his accordion.

"I'm popular in America. I married a half breed. People don't like her. They like me. I don't work, just dance and play. I taught my little girl to play. She's a quarter breed. A loaf of breed my family." (laughs)

When I have gas I remember my wound. I call myself Samuel or David when I perform.

Wrapped me like a pharaoh when I die. I'm Belgian.

He taught his little girl, Virginia, to laugh. His little Belgium chocolate, his little girl.

SELF-DIRECTED MOVIES

HOW TO DO IT
In this technique you are the director. You set the stage, call in the performers and enjoy the humor and pathos from your job well done.

Before you begin, decide:

WHERE:	Where is it you would like the scene to take place. (ie Egypt, the old west, England)
WHEN:	Is it the 1900's? Prehistoric times? The future? Name the year or era.
WHO:	An American Indian? Cleopatra of the Nile? Your great-grandfather?
WHAT:	Is there any specific message I would like the movie to transmit to me?

And begin.

MUSIC

GET COMFORTABLE

Close your eyes. Touch your thumb and forefinger together on one hand. Get comfortable. Let your breathing be easy and relaxed.

BLESS ME

> Bless me on all levels
> Physically, mentally
> Emotionally and spiritually
> So I may truly
> recognize and fulfill my life's purpose.
> Let all teachings be for the highest good
> of myself and humanity.
> Help me reconnect
> with my special gifts
> and let me lovingly shed any
> negative messages given by insensitive people.
>
> Thank you.
> Amen.

PICTURE YOUR SETTING

Imagine your chosen setting in its entirety. Picture all the colors and shapes, the smells, use all your senses. Look out on the horizon. Look at the earth. Notice the sky.

GIVE IT A TITLE

Picture and imagine the name of this movie coming across the screen of your mind. Call up the first thing that comes to you, don't censor it.

CALL IN THE ACTORS

Bring the performers into your scene. Dress them as you see fit. Again don't think, interpret, or analyze. Let them be.

ACTION

When you have a clear setting and characters, call for action and let the play begin.

WATCH THE MOVIE

Take a nice deep breath and enjoy.

RETAKES

As you watch the presentation, if you are upset, displeased or unsatisfied with the outcome, you say "RETAKE" and run the scene over again. A wonderful way to do this is to go back to a place of pain or conflict and run the movie with the subtitle of "The Best Possible Outcome". You may run the scene as many times as you like until you are satisfied. This is an excellent way to come to a peaceful resolving of physical and emotional pain in your present life. It is a form of subconscious "reframing" or reordering control over negative feelings.

ASK QUESTIONS

- **Feet?**   Look at your feet. This will ground you. Describe what you see Notice if you have shoes.

- **Clothes?**   Notice what you are wearing or not wearing.

- **Senses?**   One by one, allow your experience to enter each of your senses. Notice any smells, tastes, sounds, bodily sensations, sights and extra sensory sensations.

- **Others?**   Are you alone or with someone?

- **Location?**   Are you inside or outside?

- **Time?**   What is the time period or year? What season is it?

- **Experience?**   What is happening? What happens next?

- **Death?**   Answer the question: "How did this entity die?"

- **White Light**   Send that entity white light. Picture and imagine a flood of white light upon them and see what happens.

- **Learned?**   "What have I learned from this lifetime" or "What message is this entity wishing to give me?"

COME ON BACK AND OPEN YOUR EYES

GROUND YOURSELF

EXAMPLE USING SELF-DIRECTED MOVIE APPROACH

Yuriko in Yokohama

Where: Japan
When: 200 years ago
Who: Someone very wise
What: To explore any connection with Japan.

Young Samurai Speaks:
A teahouse. A tatami. Water with koi. A lump under the tatami in the corner. I never put it down smoothly enough. Just like rocks in the garden - perfectly imperfect. They wanted to fix it - the funny man who laid it down. I like it that way.

I wear a tight obi and sword. Strong cord of silk. My sword has silken threads, black and white in a checkered pattern. My shoes are wooden with red brocade.

Geisha Speaks:
I see an old man. He has a long, long moustache and beard. He is old. His hair is white. He is very powerful. They call him the great samurai yet he has no sword. He is the samurai of the garden of words. The samurai who writes the truth. He speaks for the emperor. The humble orator of the great emperor. Some believe that he has a mind of the emperor tucked neatly within his own mind. His sentences are short and clean. Brush on silk - stroke words. These ring like the bell of the great temple in Yokohama. Many carvings of angels. Great tall statues.

Yuriko. I am geisha to the great Emperor and orator. I wear white tabi and wooden shoes. Blue and black. My kimono is blue and purple with a large white stork. My obi has many layers - yellow, white, mustard, blue, purple. I wear silk cords to show my position.

I sit in the corner of the teahouse behind the shoji wall, behind the rice screen. I serve sake. I have studied tea ceremony. I like the tea. It is green and grainy.

I like my humble master. We are one great river flowing - flowing through time together. Graceful as silk ribbons across the land of my parents and my parent's parents.

I have a girl child. No, she died. It was very sad. My tears joined the river. I wear purple for her. The yellow for the egg broken. She was never full born. Perhaps she only visited in a dream.

The fabric of the blood was not soiled for a long 3 months or more and there was a deep pain I felt in the night, a cold night, and I was very, very hot. I squatted in the snow. The tiniest of dolls was born. I kissed her and smelled her. She was perfect. Her cord was like the silk cord I wear. There is no place for tears in the bloodied snow of the doll. Her eyes do not open. They are large and closed. I want to open them but I kiss them instead. A wolf could eat her. Where will I take her? I would like to take it to my master but I cannot. I will throw her into the river. There is great questioning in the village. A frozen baby is found in the river. Whose baby is it? No on knows. The river knows.

Sepuku. Master was very angry. She brought shame when she threw the baby in the river. Bring shame. "You are no better than women of the village who eat their babies" he said to her. I do not know who the father is.

(send her the light) She dies in the fetus position.
She flies like a great stork, a great white
stork on wings of clouds. Waves of wings.
Very beautiful. Very welcome.

(what did this entity teach you?)
Shame, self-punishment and peace.

RETAKE: "THE BEST POSSIBLE OUTCOME"

Yuriko. She is very gentle. A quiet lady. She is very polite. She loves the samurai. He is much older. It is his baby. She wears a kimono the color of koi. Moving in and out. The yellow koi is moving in and out of her kimono. There is a little teahouse on her kimono.

Her belly hurt very much the day and night of the doll. She goes to the snow to drop the baby but the baby does not come. She comes back to the teahouse. Her master is meeting with three men. One man is fat with brown cheeks like oranges. She waits behind the shoji, quietly. He calls her in to pour sake and sees her eyes and asks the men to leave. They understand.

"What is wrong, Yuriko?" he asks.

"I have deep pain from the child." she says.

"Oh my, a child is to be born. Why have you not told me?"

"I was afraid"

"It is a time to rejoice. I am old. I have no child. This child will become me when I depart. I welcome the child. You are to rest so the child can be born. I will have two servant girls beside you." And he gives her sake from his cup. "You hold the flower and the light within you. You must rest so the flower will bloom. Precious. And tomorrow's light. Rest."

She feels tears in the corners of her eyes. She doesn't want to cry but she cannot help it. Her tears wet her wig, roll behind her eyes. He lays beside her and falls to sleep.

She spend quiet days. She is making a kimono, blue and yellow flowers. A yellow flower for the new baby. A flower upon the earth, blooming on the land. And she bore him like a flower, a crying flower. A boy baby who brings much joy to the heart of her lord, the samurai.

She learns patience and love and she is quiet and gentle.

painting by Shelley Lessin Stockwell

CHAPTER 9

CHANNELING:
TUNE IN YOUR OWN CHANNEL

Some people love to pay a visit and lots of money to someone who sets themselves up to be a channel. They swear that channeling is the greatest. And it can be. Being your own channel is even more fun!

Here is a way to receive your own information. It is like going to a private movie and it only costs you a little time and a lot of wonderment.

HOW TO DO IT

MUSIC
Put on gentle music.

TAPE RECORDER
Turn on another tape recorder to capture your words if you desire.

BLESS ME

Bless me on all levels
Physically, mentally

Emotionally and spiritually
So I may truly
recognize and fulfill my life's purpose.
Let all teachings be for the highest good
of myself and humanity.
Help me reconnect
with my special gifts
and let me lovingly shed any
negative messages given by insensitive people.

Thank you.
Amen.

BLUE

Say the word "blue" and close your eyelids

EYELOCK

Relax your eyelids so much that they don't feel like opening. When you've done a good job of playing this game with your eyelids, test them only to discover that they don't feel like opening.

BLUE AGAIN

Now that you've tested your eyelids and they stayed closed say "blue" again.

TRAVEL TO ANOTHER TIME

Invite images to appear on the movie screen of your mind. Images may "appear" as energy, taste, smell, vision or touch. Don't sensor or monitor or analyze. Simply experience your movie and allow the past to present itself. Take your time. If you obsess on a present situation say "Go back in time, farther back". Don't worry if you think you are making up the story. It doesn't even need to make sense. Just let it come forward.

Note: If, at first, you see only black or patterns, report them. I like to report everything out loud and tape record what I say.

COME ON BACK

When you are ready to return to your here and now awareness, take a deep breath and stretch.

OPEN YOUR EYES

Ground yourself by using one of the methods described in "Rules of the Road".

EXAMPLES USING CHANNELING:

Autistic Child — Lorraine (1986)

Purple and blue over to the left. Like something pleated like drapes. Velvet shapes. Fragments of shapes. Carriage. Brocade on it. Looks like a carriage - a horse drawn carriage - no horse - purple velvet. It may not be real, it fades there and not there.

I think I am in the kitchen - the carriage is outside. I'm in the kitchen. Big stones, big round stones like big bellies. I'm by the wooden benches. Tree logs cut in half. The table is a big slab of wood. Lots of niches and holes. I've got white linen shoes tied on with linen - very small feet - a child. I have little legs. I feel little. I have little hips; have a little tummy; and I don't have a chest. A bonnet on - white linen with a little yellow; pink roses around top. I look all frothy, lots of white linen around. I want to go in the carriage.

But she can't. She's depressed, she's in the kitchen. She's not happy. She doesn't look up at anybody. She feels like she has feathers stuffed all around - stuffed - all that linen. Suffocated - very depressed. She doesn't talk.

The kitchen doesn't smell like anything except stone. A fat lady works in the kitchen: Rebecca. She has a hat that looks like a mushroom with lace on the edges. Curly brown hair, she has a fat face , little teeny eyes. She likes to cook....

The little girl is lonely, the little girl feels paralyzed. Maybe she is. Nothing moves on her. Her legs just hang there. She wants to go in the carriage because she can't move but the   carriage doesn't have a horse so it's like her legs. They can't move. Stuck; in the kitchen with Rebecca - stuffed - she can't barely breathe.

She feels good when man touches her. Man has big hands with hair. Makes her comfortable - got a big black beard (it's master again - only a little different) He always puts his hand on her heart and pets her head and she can't move. Someone said it's because her mother didn't want her. She thinks it's something she was born with. She couldn't kick as a baby. Nothing worked. She couldn't even cry or talk when she was a baby. Everyone carried her. Now the big man, and Rebecca touch her. Big man is Gregory - Uncle Gregory. He has dirt under his fingernails - he farms the land and he loves her. He knows all about her and he knows her mother very well. Might be her father but he's called Uncle Gregory.

I'm very depressed in this gaule. I can't move. I want to get out of here. Want to go in the carriage and look at the road and trees. I want to get out of here. I don't hear very well either. I smell very well. No food in the kitchen to smell - just earth and stones - stones like bellies. So depressed - that's all there is to me.

I like purple - reminds me of the carriage. I like to live with Gregory forever. He loves me. He touches me everyday. Everyday he comes into lunch to be with me.

(How do you feel about yourself?)
Awful, I can't do anything. I'm a lump.

(Do you love yourself?)
I don't think so. I can't move. I can't speak. I don't hear too well. I see colors. I see/feel people touch me.

(Do you touch others? Speak?)
No, my arms don't work. I can drool. I don't like to drool. I have pains that travel in my body. Now in my side sometimes in my head.

(What did you learn in this lifetime?)
The power of solitude. Victim. I had to learn the other side of power. I'm not doing well.

(How did you die?)
I choke on vomit in bed. A big bed. We must be rich. Wooden poster and lots of velvet - tall. They pick me up and put me in it and I die there.

Autistic Child – Lorraine (1990)

Lorraine - girl with pain in her feet and legs even though they don't work. She can't speak and can't hear. Once when a big man was playing with her, he tossed her on the big bed and she accidental fell off the side. It hurt. (I relived her death again.)

CHAPTER 10

DREAM REGRESSIONS

"To sleep, perchance to dream"
—-William Shakespeare

The Senois people used the power of sleep and dreaming as a valuable tool for themselves and their loving society. Patricia Garfield popularized their approach to working out conflicts. In her book <u>Creative Dreaming</u>, images from dreams present you powerful symbology, guides and images for a happier life.

Carlos Castineda, in his famous books about the Indian Wiseman, Don Juan, also talked about learning as you sleep.

To use the sleep state you must make sure that you keep a pencil and paper by your bed and make a decision to write down the images. Dream regressions have a sly way of slipping back into the subconscious. I think that it is a good idea to practice writing down dream images for several nights before you begin your sleep regression journey. As soon as you awaken, write down your dreams. Let your pencil write even if it doesn't make a lot of sense to you.

The process of dream regressions improves with practice.

HOW TO DO IT

PENCIL AND PAPER

Have a pencil and paper next to your bed.

BEFORE YOU SLEEP

Get comfortable in your bed and before going to sleep, tell yourself "Tonight as I sleep, I will go back in time, back to a past life and I will remember my vision. When I awake I will write it down."

THE JOURNEY: THE GIFT

While you are dreaming, you get to be creative. (This is not as difficult as you may think) If you find yourself reliving a frightening moment, DON'T WAKE UP. Simply finish the moment. Let's say you are being chased by a bear and he's about to jump on you ... let him. If you die (this is the fun part) ask him for a gift. You will be thrilled by what you receive. Or you might find that you kill the bear. Ask the dead bear for a gift!

WRITE IT DOWN

Then wake up and write the vision down. Draw your gift if you like. If there is someone with you, you can tell them your regression and that will help you remember it.

Most importantly, answer this question: What did I learn about myself from this vision?

Keep all these notes. Don't throw them away. When you review them in the months that follow, you will be astounded by your sleep messages.

EXAMPLES USING DREAM REGRESSIONS:

I am particularly good at dreaming into the future. The power of these progressions always astounds me.

My Father's Death - 1967

In the months that followed my father's death, I had the same dream on several nights. My father was playing tennis (in real life, my father never played tennis). He suddenly fell over. There was great chaos. Everyone rushed to him saying: "Oh my God he's dead." I looked at him. He looked up, opened one eye and winked at me and said (so no one else could hear) "I am not really dead Shelley. They think I am but I'm not really dead".

Seventeen years later, my father's law partner, John Foley was playing tennis. He suddenly fell over and went into a coma. He remained in that state (not really dead) for several weeks, before he finally departed. I was in the right church but the wrong pew.

My Father's Death - 1967

In the months following my father's death, I wrote down this dream:

I was sitting in a bleacher which looked like a reviewing stand and my father sat up in his coffin and said to me: "Shelley, I'm not really dead, I have a gift for you" and he gave me a pyramid made of a substance like nothing I have ever seen on the earth plane. Each surface of the pyramid had a hologram like image of different body parts. One side was an eye, another an arm, and another a heart.

It is my belief that this gift (clearly a very personal gift to stimulate my awareness and growth) brought me back to ancient Egypt and served as a personal rosetta stone of time travel and respect for the human form.

Since this dream progression/ regression I have become a successful portrait and time travel specialist.

painting by Shelley Lessin Stockwell

CHAPTER 11

SPECIAL EFFECTS

Special effects enhance and focus your journey, helping you to clarify, understand, resolve, and put to rest unresolved relationships, pain, and limiting attitudes. In this chapter you will learn how to Track people, physical discomforts, and attitudes; Idiomotor Self-talk; and the Telepathy Game for two.

TRACKING ANOTHER INTO A PAST LIFE

It is extremely useful to explore significant relationships back in time. Often you are left with a clarification of how and why your present relationship works the way it does. You may track a beloved or someone you have strong negative feelings for. You can track anyone living or dead. You can even track animals!

HOW TO DO IT

MUSIC
Put on some nice soft music.

BLESS ME

Bless me on all levels
Physically, mentally
Emotionally and spiritually
So I may truly
recognize and fulfill my life's purpose.
Let all teachings be for the highest good
of myself and humanity.
Help me reconnect
with my special gifts
and let me lovingly shed any
negative messages given by insensitive people.

Thank you.
Amen.

ESTABLISH VIBRATIONS
Establish your vibrations and the vibrations of your significant other.

Now that you know you own energy frequency, or vibration,you notice that your vibration is different from any one else.

DECIDE WHO TO TRACK
Close your eyes and think of the person you would like to track. Feel their unique vibration.

TRAVEL TO ANOTHER TIME
Choose any journey technique and go into the past, back into another place in time where you find your vibration and that other person's distinct vibration. Notice whatever comes up. Let it flow. Use all your senses.

Focus on the connection you have with that person in that place.

COME ON BACK
When you are ready to return to your here and now awareness, take a deep breath and stretch.

OPEN YOUR EYES
Ground yourself by using one of the methods described in"Rules of the Road".

Once you know you have had an earlier connection with that person, you will better understand your relationship with them in the future. Also, you will understand that if they pass on before you (in this lifetime), you can release them with love, knowing that you are able to reconnect with their energy simply by closing your eyes and recalling their energy in the past, the present, or projected into the future (progression).

EXAMPLE OF TRACKING ANOTHER

I chose to track my younger brother Marc Lessin because I have had a difficult time with him during this lifetime. I have also felt very loving and maternal toward him. He is 10 years younger than I. When my mother died, he sued both me and our older brother, Alex, over her estate. His posture was, and is, that my mother's money belonged to him, not to Alex or myself. Here is what happened when I tracked Marc:

Jenny #1
(Using Idiomotor Induction)

My name is Jenny. I'm a very thin and weak little girl. Picnic blanket. Green hills in Wales. Jenny Donahue. White smock top, dark bodice and laces on bodice. Dark skirt. Brown leather shoes. My father made them. Garren O'Donnell is my lover. (My younger brother Marc from this lifetime now)

Note: This session was interrupted by someone ringing my door bell. Three hours latter, I began again...right where I left off!

Jenny #2

Jenny is very thin, very fragile like a bird. She has brown shoes made of leather. Her father made them. She has on white stockings and a garter and white bloomers and a lace bodice. She is by a tree with nuts that fall down. She has a big straw hat with a brim, a ribbon and little flowers on it. Her aunty Gram made it for her. Her legs don't work. She has to be carried and put places. She is 16 years old. Her legs are like sticks. Jeremy Wiscott is her dad. He sexually abused her. He got drunk and said she wasn't good for anything else because of her legs. She became very timid after that. She loves her dad very much.

She is sharing a peach or an apricot with her male friend. He is clumsy with a big adam's apple and pimples. He likes her. She is very timid. They came in a black carriage for a drive. It is his father's carriage, he can't afford it. They are in the livery business. They are very rich. He doesn't like his pimples. Either does she. I like the apricot and the grass. I like your voice. I like your kindness. I don't like your pimples. "I want to marry you", he says. She cries "I can't marry you, my legs don't work. My father is already done with me." "I don't care about your father. I will spit in his face", he says. "Don't do that."

Her father killed him. He hit him over the head with an andiron. He asked for her hand and he hit him over the head and killed him. That's how my grandmother got her skinny legs. (That is why Shelley's grandmother, Esther, had skinny legs, she to had something wrong with her legs.) Her friend was Marc (Shelley's brother now) He died before he could get his father's money. That is why my brother sued me - to get all my mother's money. He thinks it is his right. She marries someone else with red hair and freckles. His name is Gregory. He is a jolly lad. They had 3 babies - Karen, Claudette, and Binky. Benjamin is his real name but they call him Binky. Broderick is their last name. She outlives her husband. She loves him very much. He was in the wool business. She cooked a lot of pork.

She died at the age of 54. She got crushed on a rock wall. It was an accident. Gray and blue rocks. The rock wall crumbled and fell on her. She died under the rocks. She couldn't move. she was very scared. One rock hit her head and she was unconscious right away. She was in a carriage and the horses ran too fast.

She left her body through her heart and an angel took her by the hand and she walked to heaven.

She learned forgiveness. She was peaceful. She learned forgiveness.

TRACKING A PHYSICAL DISCOMFORT

As you follow the simple instructions in this book, you too can "clear" away pain by going to the source of that pain.

It is interesting to note that if you describe a pain or discomfort in a certain "turn of phrase", for example, you might say: "my back is killing me", you will be fascinated to discover that your choice of words will perfectly reflect the onset of that pain. Perhaps, you died when your back was broken or perhaps you broke someone else's back. You get the idea. Thought becomes words and form. What is often called "thought forms" literally manifests itself in a physical form.

HOW TO DO IT

DESCRIBE THE PAIN

Write down a description of the pain. For example: "I have a pain in my neck. The pain just kills me."

MUSIC

Put on some nice soft music.

BLESS ME

> Bless me on all levels
> Physically, mentally
> Emotionally and spiritually
> So I may truly
> recognize and fulfill my life's purpose.
> Let all teachings be for the highest good
> of myself and humanity.
> Help me reconnect
> with my special gifts
> and let me lovingly shed any
> negative messages given by insensitive people.
>
> Thank you.
> Amen.

PLACE YOUR HAND ON THE PAIN IF POSSIBLE.
STATE YOUR PURPOSE.

CHOOSE ANY MODE OF EXPLORATION

Go back in time, where it all began, the source of this discomfort. Take a deep breath, let it out and report the first thing that comes to mind. Don't think. Don't analyze.

ASK QUESTIONS

- **Feet?**   Look at your feet. This will ground you. Describe what you see Notice if you have shoes.

- **Clothes?**   Notice what you are wearing or not wearing.

- **Senses?**   One by one, allow your experience to enter each of your senses. Notice any smells, tastes, sounds, bodily sensations,sights and extra sensory sensations.

- **Others?**   Are you alone or with someone?

- **Location?**   Are you inside or outside?

- **Time?**   What is the time period or year? What season is it?

- **Experience?** What is happening? What happens next?

- **Death?**   Answer the question: "How did this entity die?"

- **White Light** Send that entity white light. Picture and imagine a flood of white light upon them and see what happens.

- **Learned?**   "What have I learned from this lifetime" or "What message is this entity wishing to give me?"

THE HEALING BEGINS

Say: "I am choosing to release this experience, person and the pain from my body".

RELEASING AND HEALING

Have a conversation with the part that hurts you. For example, say: "Neck, you have my full attention, so tell me what it is you want me to know". See what your neck tells you. "Give me simple, clear things that I may do to make you feel better".

Now decide which thing you are willing to do and tell your neck. "Neck, Thank you for getting my attention and now that you have I agree to do the things you request and since I have agreed to do them - stop it. You don't need to get my attention any more".

COME ON BACK

When you are ready to return to your here and now awareness, take a deep breath and stretch.

OPEN YOUR EYES

Ground yourself by using one of the methods described in "Rules of the Road'.

EXAMPLE - TRACKING A PHYSICAL DISCOMFORT

On this journey, I choose to explore bladder infections.

Zebadaya Marcus Quinton

I see red flashes, green grass, shapes, squared off rectangular shapes. Blues. It is the sky, big and long, across flatlands with clouds sweeping up. A dog is running across the earth. Little yippie dog. Brown ears, dirty white, with brown splotches. Wagon - old buckboard. Splinters. There are splinters on the part of the wood where you put your feet. Rusted metal. Bad shoes, ugly shoes; Bowed on the tips. Zebadaya Marcus Quinton. Old top hat. Dirty. Not a clean fellow old Zeb. Doesn't bathe very often. Horses are dirty. Houses are dirty. Dust everywhere. Zeb is not into cleanliness. Zeb is into chewing tobacco.

No, not chewing tobacco, snuff! What kind of fool would not know the difference between chewing tobacco and snuff. Women are dumb. My mom was dumb as a dog. No, dogs is smarter that mom, except when he chases porcupines. But he learns. Women drive you crazy. Nag, nag, nag. Never clean enough. Never nice enough. Never clean enough. Drove my dad half mad. My dad was Justin Zachariah. My sister is Becky. Becky Elizabeth. Rebecca Elizabeth really. She puts her hands on her hips just like mother. Nag, nag, nag. "Why don't you feed the chickens. Why don't you shine the shoes up. Go take care of the goat." Becky wears a little blue checkered dress with a white apron.

Terrible cramps. (Just like Shelley's bladder discomfort) Don't know what is wrong. Dr. Jarvis, he came by. Roving around in my belly. Said "Eh boy, you got some cramps. Some goose fat will straighten you right up."

They are letting my blood out. Cut my ankle. Goose grease, blood letting: dumbest thing. Where did the doctor go to school? With those damn indians? They always cut people.

Jesus is coming over the mountain, through the sky. Arms are outstretched. Light is coming through his hands. Jesus loves all the children. Jesus shines his light on me. Follows me to the little church. Somebody died. It was me. I died and I got my top hat on, lying here in this coffin. Jesus smiles on me. Jesus don't care about dirt none. There's still dirt on the inside on my hat.

My heart stopped. Hurt mighty awful 'til I saw Jesus. 'Til I saw Jesus. His face is an angel. That beard in the pictures is just a mask. He has a face of lights. No beard when there is lights. Spinning, spinning lights.

Asthma

Several years ago, I was speaking to a Rotary club when a elder gentleman asked me if I did past life regressions. "I've dabbled in it", I replied. Two months later, this gentleman was in my office. During my pre-interview I asked him about his health.

"I've been plagued with asthma my entire life", he replied.

"How's your memory?"

"Very good", he said. And he shared with me a recall he had when he was five years old.

"What do you know about past life regressions," I asked.

"Nothing", he said "I'm simply curious."

"Have you ever read anything about regressions?" I asked.

"No, I've only heard it could be done".

"Fine", I thought. Hypnotherapy is a fantastic tool to eliminate the symptoms of asthma. I was looking forward to teaching my technique for "turning off asthma". This gentle, retired aerospace engineer, in his gray suit, closed his eyes and embarked on such a monumental past life journey that it has had me doing them ever since. Over the years, I have refined my techniques, have done hundreds of sessions, and have never stopped being in awe of the vast imagining and healing power of our creative subconscious mind.

His session went something like this:

"Go back to a place in time, in this lifetime, when you are very young".

"How old are you?", I asked him and a tearful, little voice answered
"I'm two."

"What is going on?"
"It's the day before Christmas and I want to open my presents. My daddy won't let me. He says I have to wait until Christmas comes."

And the man on my sofa launched into a monumental asthma attack.

"Great" I thought and I carefully showed him how to "turn off" his asthma.

"Go back farther", I said. "Go back to an earlier place in time."
The man on my sofa became still and silent, emerging into a state known as a catatonic trance. After several moments, I noticed that his hands were twitching.

"What do you have in your hand" I asked.
"An auger."

"What do you do with it?", I asked.
"I run it across the stones".

"Where are the stones?"
"In the courtyard"

"Where do you live?"
"In Rome." This man, now an eight year old Greek boy, told the details of his life in Rome. He presented vivid accounts of his life: his clothes, his toys, his food, his religion, his friends. His mother was a cold socialite, his father, an orator.

"I am learning to write. I write on the tablets and with sticks in the sand."
"Here is a stick" I said handing him paper and a pencil. And he began to write in Greek. It seems that this boy grew up to be a man, a good man, who never married, nor did he fully get over his mother's rejection. Yet, he went on to change the course of boating. Sea faring vessels had been wide and he created a narrow boat and took many people to islands off of Italy.

"How did he die?" I asked.
"When he was forty he went to an island where there were elephants and he was crushed by an elephant". At this time the engineer on my sofa launched into the most awful asthma attack I have ever witnessed.

"Take a deep breath I said. "Turn off your asthma" And he did.
Thus, a three hour past life regression session came to a close.

Several years later I called up this gentleman. "Do you remember me?" I asked.
"Do I remember you. You changed my life. That boy is me. I have carried him with me my whole life and I feel a great sense of peace having reunited with him once again. As for my asthma, I've never had another attack. I had a couple of instances when I felt tightness, but I simply took a deep breath and turned it off."

TRACKING AN ATTITUDE OR BEHAVIOR

HOW TO DO IT
     If you have identified an attitude or behavior that gets in the way of your happiness and fulfillment, this is a splendid way to cleanse it.

WRITE DOWN THE LIMITING ATTITUDE OR BEHAVIOR

MUSIC

BLESS ME

> Bless me on all levels
> Physically, mentally
> Emotionally and spiritually
> So I may truly
> recognize and fulfill my life's purpose.
> Let all teachings be for the highest good
> of myself and humanity.
> Help me reconnect

with my special gifts
and let me lovingly shed any
negative messages given by insensitive people.

Thank you.
Amen.

STATE YOUR PURPOSE
"I am choosing to explore my (for example) over reaction to high places, or my district of people wearing pink robes or my compulsive eating or my depressed and negative outlook on life.

CHOOSE ANY MODE OF EXPLORATION

GO BACK TO A RECENT TIME
Go back to the most recent time you experienced that attitude or behavior. Recall it in vivid clarity using each of your senses.

GO BACK TO THE SOURCE OF THIS BELIEF OR ATTITUDE
Go back in time, where it all began, the source of this discomfort. Take a deep breath, let it out and report the first thing that comes to mind. Don't think. Don't analyze.

ASK QUESTIONS

• Feet?	Look at your feet. This will ground you. Describe what you see Notice if you have shoes.
• Clothes?	Notice what you are wearing or not wearing.
• Senses?	One by one, allow your experience to enter each of your senses. Notice any smells, tastes, sounds, bodily sensations,sights and extra sensory sensations.
• Others?	Are you alone or with someone?
• Location?	Are you inside or outside?
• Time?	What is the time period or year? What season is it?
• Experience?	What is happening? What happens next?
• Death?	Answer the question: "How did this entity die?"
• White Light	Send that entity white light. Picture and imagine a flood of white light upon them and see what happens.
• Learned?	"What have I learned from this lifetime" or "What message is this entity wishing to give me?"

COME ON BACK

When you are ready to return to your here and now awareness, take a deep breath and stretch.

OPEN YOUR EYES

Ground yourself by using one of the methods described in "Rules of the Road".

EXAMPLE - TRACKING AN ATTITUDE

Nicoli

I see a Russian wolf hound. I wanted to go up the hill, wanted to go up but I just come down again. It is a brown wolf hound. White face, eyes like a coyote. It is on a hunt. It is on a hunt.

It is cold. Bitter cold. Red cosack. Red coat. Red waist coat. Black trim. Not the fir trim, not long fir. Short curly fir. Black buttons. It is Alexander the Great. Tsar - Great Tsar of Russia. He holds a whip in his hands. He is not real. He is the great Tsar, great tsar. I must not say it but the Great Alexander is a filthy slob. He's a swine. He's a big man with fat hips, dirty fingernails, filth. My room is very cold - this black room. I have gray stringy hair, leather shoes, and I am in charge of the closet of Alexander the Great, the great tsar. The swine. He's thick in the body and thick in the mind. He makes me thick. Cold and thick. His clothes are thicker than mine. His shoes are thicker. Sometimes I put on his royal robes and I am warm.

I despise him - swine. My father and mother were sent away. They thought it was an honor to spend my days in a cold room watching the wardrobe of a filthy swine.

Sometimes I climb upon ladies in the court - chambermaids. They laugh. I slap them. I had my way with one. Her bowed hat draped in pearls. A regal lady she was. The wolf hound tore her to shreds. Bit her on the neck. Maybe it was me. I am a wolf hound. Maybe it was me. I bit her in the name of the great tsar of Russia - the great mighty swine - Alexander.

My penis is large. I am a wolf hound. I am more kingly, more tsarly, more magnificent than the royal highness. "Sir" I say, "Here's your waistcoat. Enjoy the hunt." Perhaps the wolf hounds will tear him to shreds and I will have the robes to myself. My room has one candle and much dust.

His name is Nicoli. It is winter. There is snow and the ground is frozen. They go out and hunt in the snow. Nicoli is always cold. He went to work for the tsar when he was six. Now he is 31. He will not live past 36. He will die of a fever in the mind. It will be a bad death but no one will notice. He has no friends.

Gray stringy hair. Dark brown skin. His hair is to his shoulders. He wears a forest green weskit (waistcoat). His pants are brown and baggy. His shoes are very ugly. His hands are fat and small. You can say he is very nice looking. His beady eyes are strange.

(send him the light)

He never grew up. He still felt like the boy whose parents abandoned him. Alexander was cruel to him. I guess he doesn't want the light.

(what did this entity teach you) Hatred. Lust. I learned to be afraid of dogs. I always had a phobia of dog's teeth.

Note: Alexander I, Emperor of Russia, lived from 1777 - 1825
         Alexander II, also Emperor of Russia lived 1818 - 1881

IDIOMOTOR CONVERSATIONS (IDEA-MOTOR SKILLS)

This approach is like having a direct-line communication through your central nervous system. Your subconscious mind will speak to you though the central nervous system and bypass your clever and manipulative conscious thinking.

In this approach, you will establish responses for the words "yes", "no", and "don't know, don't want to say". What emerges as your expression for those words will be for each individual journey. Each time you do this approach, you must reestablish your idiomotor signals as your body may communicate in different ways at different times. Idiomotor conversations can be done sitting in a chair, in bed before you sleep at night, almost anytime and anyplace where you would like to have a word with yourself.

HOW TO DO IT

MUSIC
Put on some nice soft music. Decide what you would like to know, understand, or resolve.

BLESS ME

> Bless me on all levels
> Physically, mentally
> Emotionally and spiritually
> So I may truly
> recognize and fulfill my life's purpose.

Let all teachings be for the highest good
of myself and humanity.
Help me reconnect
with my special gifts
and let me lovingly shed any
negative messages given by insensitive people.

Thank you.
Amen.

BREATH DEEPLY

Take a deep, cleansing breath

ESTABLISHING "YES"

Say "yes" again and again in your mind. Let the energy express itself in a physical movement such as the twitching of a finger or lip, any part of the body that moves in response to the word "yes".

ESTABLISHING "NO"

Same as "establishing yes"

ESTABLISH "DON'T KNOW, DON'T WANT TO SAY"

Same as "Establishing 'yes'".

ASK QUESTIONS

Take a full breath. Ask the questions you would like to know more about. Example: Is the source of my neck pain from something that happened in this lifetime? Is there some information that I can look at so I may resolve the pain? will you take me to the source of the pain.

BEGIN YOUR JOURNEY

Go back in time (or forward). Allow whatever comes up to emerge. If any past life images come up, ask the following questions:

• What time of the year it is.

• Are you inside or outside?

• Alone or with someone?

• Look at your feet. (This will ground you and bring you clearly and vividly into this space and time)

• One by one, allow your experience to enter each of your senses. Notice any smells. Notice any tastes. Notice any sounds.

- What is the time period or year?

- What is happening?

- Answer the question: "How did this entity die?"

- Send that entity white light. Picture and imagine a flood of white light upon them and see what happens.

- Answer the question: "What have I learned from this lifetime" or "What message is this entity wishing to give me?"

THE TELEPATHY GAME FOR TWO

PHASE ONE

Sit down facing a friend. Decide who is going to go first. If you are the one going first, close your eyes and "get centered". A good way to do that is to put yourself in your very most favorite place in your imagination. When you are ready and feel centered, nod your head so your partner can give you your assignment.

Now it is time for your partner to say the name, age, and location of another living person, preferably someone you do not know.

You now report any visions, images, thoughts or awarenesses that come to you. If they are accurate, your partner will say "That fits with my information" or they will say "That doesn't fit with my information" if you are way off base. You will be stunned at how accurate this simple telepathy exercise works and it usually gets even better with repetition.

PHASE TWO:

Arrange with a friend that on a particular day, place, and time, that you will both take ten minutes, close your eyes and visualize a scene from your imagination. Make the scene as vivid as possible, noting any characters, smells, tastes, colors, sensations and feelings. Now open your eyes and write down your experience. Now call your friend and share what you have written. Another way to do that is to tell your friend that on an appointed time, you will send them a message and at that point in time you will think of an object, a place, a thing or a scene and you will say their name quietly in your head. Open your eyes, write it down, contact them, see if they got the message.

PHASE THREE:

Lie down next to a friend and notice your own energy. Notice the energy of your friend. Decide to go back into a past life where you and your friend had a previous connection with one another.

PUT ON NICE SOFT MUSIC.

BLESS ME

> Bless me on all levels
> Physically, mentally
> Emotionally and spiritually
> So I may truly
> recognize and fulfill my life's purpose.
> Let all teachings be for the highest good
> of myself and humanity.
> Help me reconnect
> with my special gifts
> and let me lovingly shed any
> negative messages given by insensitive people.
>
> Thank you.
> Amen.

CLEANSING BREATHS

Take deep cleansing breaths.

THE JOURNEY

Close your eyes. Watch the movie in your head. When the music ends, both of you sit up, face one another with your knees touching, and one at a time, share your experiences.

Shelley Lessin Stockwell

ABOUT THE AUTHOR

SHELLEY LESSIN STOCKWELL
*(Hypnotherapist, Motivational Speaker, Trance Channel and
International Authority on Self awareness and Success)*

Shelley Lessin Stockwell is an artist of life who believes that to live rich and lusty you must listen to your inner wisdom, respect your body, tell the truth, go for your dreams and love yourself.

She leads seminars on time travel, channeling, freedom from addictions and compulsions, joy, personal power and prosperity. Her travels have given her a chance to meet Massai warriors in Kenya, headhunters on the Amazon in Peru, scientists in the Soviet Union and royalty from Tonga. She has deep friendships with people all over the world.

Shelley holds an honorary Doctor of Divinity degree and conducts beautiful humanistic wedding ceremonies. Her newspaper columns, short stories and television show have earned her many awards.

She lives in a house overlooking the Pacific Ocean, collects turtles and likes to laugh.

*To arrange for Shelley to speak to your company, convention or organization,
write to her in care of:*
Creativity Unlimited
30819 Casilina Drive

GREAT RELATIONS:
Do-It-Yourself Counseling For Couples

by **Dr. Alex Lessin**

$9.95

Practical, easy-to-do steps for you and your beloved to grow as individuals and create more joy, zest & impact. All this in 6 easy lessons. A must for couples!

"A delightfully practical guide for the journey through the mountains and valleys of living in a relationship."

Alan Cohen, Author of:
The Dragon Doesn't Live Here Anymore

Whenever I perform a wedding I give the bride & groom my heartfelt blessings and a copy of Dr. Alex Lessin's book Great Relations."
— Alicia Bay Laurel, Weddings Made In Maui

ISBN #0-945596-00-6

SELF HYPNOSIS:
Smiles On Your Face, Money In Your Pocket

by **Shelley Lessin Stockwell**

$9.95

SOON TO BE RELEASED!

How to use it as a powerful tool for yourself, your family and your friends. Teaches you what hypnosis is & uses the untapped power of your mind to make your dreams become a reality.

Learn:
- ★ The 30 Second Zap
- ★ 42 Personal Affirmations
- ★ Hypnosis Script
- ★ Dream Charting

- ★ How to Vanish "Loser" Attitudes & Replace Them With Successful Ones
- ★ How To Be A Money Magnet

ISBN #0-912559-17-9

THE MONEY TAPE

$10.00

Created by **Dr. Joan Lessin** and **Ed Seykota,**
World famous commodities trader

Includes the workbook **The Way To Abundance"** by Dr. Alex Lessin.

"**The Money Tape was the beginning of true prosperity in my life. It helped me feel good, not only about money, but about myself and my life. I love the combination of hypnosis, 'The Money Show', and the catchy tunes.**"

— Susan Bredesen, CEO, Public Relations Firm

"**I got rid of a lot of subconscious beliefs that kept money from me,& opportunities for making money began to show up and haven't stopped.**

— Robin Johnson, Music Promoter

"**The Money Tape got me clear on my priorities and goals. It helped me see that I could create that green energy flow in many different ways.**

— Barbara Purinton, Therapist

DEEP INTO A CALMING OCEAN

$10.00

by **Allen Kaufman**

Music proven to induce Alpha State.

"**Seconds after starting your music cassette I found myself calm and relaxed . . . Thank you!** "

—Bruce Rische

SELF HYPNOSIS AUDIO CASSETTES

closed eye meditations by Shelley Lessin Stockwell   Only $10.00 each

 Lose Weight!
Lose unwanted pounds forever and gain energy and confidence.

 Yes, You Can Quit Smoking
Save money, breathe again and feel healthy.

 No More Alcohol
Break free of alcohol. Feel your life again.

 Peace and Calm
The perfect stress reducer. You need no tranquilizers.

 Yes, I Can!
Achieve your personal goals and potentials.

 No More Sugar Junkie
No more sugar blues, feel alive; terrific!

 Sleep, Beautiful Sleep
Sleep soundly and feel rested, at home or away. Good stress reduction.

 Flight Attendant Well-Being
A perfect attitude adjuster. Face passengers feeling positive, happy.

 Time Travel
Access past lives with this do-it-yourself hypnosis cassette and workbook.

Shelley Stockwell's self-hypnosis cassettes teach you to shed antiquated negative habits and replace them with the good habits you want for yourself.

Here is a sampling of the hundreds of letters we have on file:

"Thank you Shelley for giving me - ME!"   — C.M., Grand Forks, ND

"Your tapes have been a real blessing in my life"   — D.R., San Francisco, CA

"FANTASTIC! You wonderful, crazy, creative woman. Thanks for sharing so much with everyone."   — V.R., Los Angeles, CA

Self Hypnosis Cassette Tapes
60 Minutes Each

U R WHAT U EAT & THE DINOSAUR RAP

$10.00

Created by
Shelley Lessin Stockwell, Hypnotherapist
Kathy Felker, Registered Dietitian & famous puppeteer,
Betsy Moreland, Special Education Teacher,
Frank Unzuata, "The Magic Music Man"
Spike, your basic dinosaur

"U R What U Eat teaches children an important nutritional message, while providing catchy refrains. Reggae inspired embellishments make pleasant listening for adults as well and weightwatchers could use this for positive auto-suggestion." — Focus on Books

"The perfect antidote to junk food" — Judy Pastel, Mother

22 Minutes
ISBN #0-912559-14-4

MOMMY BUNNY'S GOING TO WORK

$10.00

by **Shelley Lessin Stockwell**

"A simple, reassuring song and story that can help parents enormously in dealing with their children's abandonment anxiety." — Ellen Hokanson, Focus on Books

"Before MOMMY BUNNY, Ryan threw a fit when I went to work. Now, he's happy and I don't feel guilty!" — Gayle Tritz, Flight Attendant

"Mommy rabbit left. Baby rabbit is happy and says I love you Mommy." — Suzy Brown, Age 4

ISBN #0-912559-16-0
ISBN #0-912559-06-3
(Flight Attendant Version)

Now you can play
GREAT GOLF

by **Shelley Lessin Stockwell**

**"Great Golf is a game played on a 6 inch course -
the space between your ears."** — Bobby Jones

This powerful program of "Great Golf" gets results!
You will:

✔ Improve
✔ Free your mind
✔ Build confidence
✔ Play focused and relaxed
✔ Feel your best

Daily mental and physical practice truly makes you a perfect golfer.
Your success with the Great Golf program is unlimited.

DENIAL IS NOT A RIVER IN EGYPT
Overcoming Addictions and Compulsions

by **Shelley Lessin Stockwell**

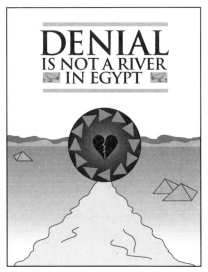

Soon to be released!

This book guides you out of the depths of depression, addiction,
compulsion and denial into the heights of self love.

Give A Friend The Gift Of Love & Laughter

Make someone happy!
Send them a book or tape today!

Give us their name, address and any greeting you wish to send and we will mail it to them from you!

To order additional gifts for friends write on the back of this order form.

To: Name _____
your friend's name

Address _____

_____
city   *state*   *zip*

My Salutation: _____

_____

Ordering Information

Please check the boxes of your choice (if more than one, please insert quantity)

Also available from Creativity Unlimited:

★ **BOOKS**

☐ INSIDES OUT..	$ 6.95
☐ GREAT RELATIONS..	9.95
☐ HYPNOSIS (Smile On Your Face & $ In Your Pocket)...............	9.95
☐ SEX & OTHER TOUCHY SUBJECTS......................	14.95
☐ GREAT GOLF	14.95
☐ DENIAL IS NOT A RIVER IN EGYPT......................	19.95
☐ TIME TRAVEL	19.95

★ **SELF HYPNOSIS CASSETTES**

☐ NO MORE SUGAR JUNKIE..........$10		☐ PEACE AND CALM $10
☐ YES, I CAN QUIT SMOKING $10		☐ YES! I CAN $10
☐ FLIGHT ATTENDANT WELL-BEING..$10		☐ LOSE WEIGHT...............$10
☐ SLEEP, BEAUTIFUL SLEEP.............$10		☐ THE MONEY TAPE $10
		☐ TIME TRAVEL $10

★ **KIDS**

☐ MOMMY BUNNY'S GOING TO WORK..............................	$10
☐ U R WHAT U EAT	$10

★ **MUSIC AND SONG**

☐ DEEP INTO A CALMING OCEAN	$10
☐ SEX & OTHER TOUCHY SUBJECTS............................	$10

SUBTOTAL

(California residents add 8.25% sales tax)
Foreign countries please add $1.00 to the price for each publication.

PLUS $2.50 POSTAGE AND HANDLING PER ITEM

TOTAL

FOR FAST ORDERING: CALL (310) 541-4844
Payment Method

☐ Check/Money Order

☐ Charge   ☐ VISA   ☐ MasterCard

Card No. _____

Expiration Date _____

_____
card holder's signature

Please complete this page and mail to: *please print*

♡ CREATIVITY UNLIMITED PRESS
30819 Casilina, Rancho Palos Verdes, CA 90274

Name _____

Address _____

_____
city   *state*   *zip*

Phone (_____) _____